Dedication

GAS,

I was honored to be your wife.

Julie and Mark,

I am blessed to be your mother.

Contents

Foreword

I am deeply honored to have been asked to write a foreword for the latest of Joyce Stedelbauer's books. As you will see, she continues to write with great insight, compassion, and wisdom. I have known Joyce and her late husband George as a couple since the mid 1950s. Many are the warm memories of time spent in their home and around their always bountiful table over the decades.

George was my oldest and dearest friend. We met as four year olds in pre-kindergarten in the basement of a Carnegie library in a small town in Southern Ontario, Canada. Our friendship continued over the years even though his family moved several times as their business as General Motors dealers flourished. George would return each summer to spend time with his Grandfather, Morley. Our mid-teen summers were times of fast cars, spirited conversation and discussion, and big band music, love of which we never outgrew. As Joyce writes, these elements remained significant in our lives.

During the 60s I drove in a number of motorsports events, including International Rallys. George, by then a successful GM dealer on his own, rode as navigator, a critical role on these events. He always approached these contests with a clear sense of adventure, good sportsmanship and fair play. As a testament to his intelligence, in over 5000 miles of intense competition he never once gave a wrong direction or made an error. As a testament to his bravery, neither did he ever flinch!

By the end of the 70s I'd enjoyed success in motor sports and in my personal business. Never a person of faith, I'd found my accomplishments to be fleeting in terms of lasting satisfaction. There was a feeling of emptiness in my life. I came to realize that the lives of George and Joyce exemplified what I was seeking, namely: peace, joy, and contentment. They had patiently explained to me the significance of their Christian faith on more than one occasion, but I didn't feel it was for me. Finally, at their home, on a winter's night in the middle of a blizzard, I gave my life to Christ! They had been praying for me for over twenty years. The Stedelbauers greatly encouraged me in my newfound faith and saw to it that I received solid mentoring and the grounding of a warm church family in my home city.

By the mid 80s I knew that I was being called into ministry. Once again, George and Joyce, always encouraging and generous, played a significant role in underwriting my training with Campus Crusade's International School of Theology. Because of my racing background I was asked to begin a chaplaincy program on the Indy race car circuit and at the Indianapolis 500. I led that for twenty-five years, and the work continues today.

The foregoing is to underscore the significance of lives consistently well-lived and their positive impact on the lives of others. Joyce's new book is remarkably timely, given the world of confusion and discord in which we currently live. Her topic, dealing with the realities of significant loss, is one that many must face. As her story is told we are reminded of the poignancy of cherished memories, yet encouraged by her means of moving on.

Chaplain Hunter B Floyd
Founding Chaplain, CART* Ministries
Chaplain, Indiana State Police (Ret)
*Championship Auto Racing Teams

Dear Reader,

Remember we were taught never to mark in a book, doodle, or write cryptic messages in the margins?

But I wrote this book for you. Please use it like a favorite recipe book where you might add or subtract something that you want to try. Another ingredient, a new spice or herb, a different presentation.

Probably you are facing some "new now" in your life. We all are just reevaluating the pandemic.

You will get ideas as you read of some adjustments you want to make.

- Take off your heart masks
- Make notes in the margins
- Underline, scratch out, highlight or even turn down corners
- Journal your thoughts. doodles and all
- Add dates

Maybe next year you will visit these pages again and see how far you've come!

Joyce

Chapter One

Batteries Not Included

When I first met George,
there were no watch batteries.

But who cared about time?

We were young and in love.
We had all the time in the world.

Now I have a battery for my watch to run.

But there is no battery to help me
run my life without George.

In the Beginning...

BEFORE silvery planets tumbled into space like dice
or stars lit the way or moons pulled tides,
time knew no memory, longing or forgiving,
color was squeezed into little paint tubes.

Fiery red---too hot to touch, blue cool enough for dawn,
yellow strong to stand in Van Gogh's haystacks,
purple hidden in mollusk shells, and elusive
green, so difficult to capture on canvas.

BEFORE wind and rain and heat grew into atmosphere
or water roiled and played together like laughter
without any salty tears or schools for fish
or ravens said nevermore or doves made peace.

Capricious sun chased rainbows over mountains,
boulders split and slid into valleys,
pebbles skipped into the sea and cocoons released
brilliant butterflies like painted silk air.

BEFORE gazelles could leap or lions roar,
even before elephants could remember,
breezes eased into breathing and wind chimes
played lullabies, trees often waved hello,
snowdrops, sunflowers and night blooming jasmine
sweetened the air, and lovers always whispered goodnight

Angel choirs sang "Alleluia"
in the beginning,
GOD.

How Did I Get Here So Quickly?

A college girl to a bride? A wife to a widow? The first Thursday I attended a little prayer group soon after my husband's burial, Dianne challenged me to please write what I was feeling, dealing with, in my new role, possibly to help someone else. I had never been "single" before. I went from my home with my mother to my new home with George. A college girl to a bride. A wife to a widow. How did I get here so quickly?

I admire and respect my friend and thanked her for the suggestion. It took me almost a year before I could even begin. But it was a nudge that I needed to try. I wrote only three poems in those first nine months. They are included. Another poet had suggested that you need a metaphor to write about some major feelings at all. I have always prized the chambered nautilus in the wondrous world of shells, and that seemed a perfect way to picture our life together. Then the summer thundered in my head pressing emotions into my favorite turquoise stone. And, as I watched Macy's parade, a vicious wind tore at the balloons and my heart.

I certainly understand that all marriages are not happy or even successful; they range from hot to cold. In fact, over fifty percent of marriages fail. My own dear parents divorced when I was twelve, so I do understand the enormity of new problems that are realities of divorce. Our society mitigates against marriage. Family stability is disappearing. Couples often avoid the legal entanglements of marriage. Many find themselves in intolerable situations. After professional counseling, it may be necessary, for sanity and security, to be independent.

Someone has said, "If the pain is gone, the love has gone." If that is true, I expect to be in emotional pain as long as I live. But I do know my husband would expect me to be strong, and to take hold of this new life capably. Our son and daughter and grandchildren enrich life beyond measure. The amazing abundance of friends who also surround me with love and kindness make this challenging new journey possible. These thoughts are some of what I have packed into this second year. My new suitcase is turquoise.

Always Wear Red

George said to his roommate on Orientation Day at Wheaton College, "Do you see that girl in red? I'm going to take her out." And he did. Friday night at the first mixer he asked me to go to Prince Castle for ice cream. We did. Four years later at graduation we said "I do," after only a few stops and starts. Chicago was our proving ground.

We learned to be avid sightseers on his salary from the gas station. We walked many magnificent miles, tried all varieties of ethnic foods, haunted the museums, especially the art gallery guarded by the famous lions. We memorized the skyline from the planetarium.

Dreaming of "far-away places with strange sounding names" he would say, "You plan and I'll pay." I replied, "That's the best offer anyone ever made me." He loved to say, "Stick with me, kid," and I did for sixty-four years, two terrific children and their wonderful spouses, five brilliant grands, one adorable great. Memorable days, in a busy business life, exciting adventures, living both in Canada and the U.S.

International travel has been a tremendous blessing. George served on a number of service boards with overseas projects. We often were privileged to assess how staff and funds were being maximized. Some places were frightening, difficult, challenging, but we grasped a better understanding of this amazing and often beautiful planet. "Our love was here to stay." "Fly me to the moon." "How do you keep the music playing?" Until last year, 2019, suddenly a very brief hospital stay, and he was on his way without me.

What now? "When your lover has gone." "I'll see you again." "Because He (Christ) lives, I can face tomorrow." Our son's family, here in town, has gone above and beyond for me. Our daughter calls every night, and her western family sends love and surprise visits. Loving neighbors and Bible study friends surround me.

Blessed with several pastors, one fighting for his young life, and my priest friend Kathie, they help show me the way forward. She has been widowed for six years, and we are learning to "Lean on Jesus finding more power than we ever dreamed." Joan, alone two years, now a vibrant redhead sings a new song to me on her morning calls. "You are my sunshine," "It's a lovely day today, so whatever you've got to do…" And we often did it together until the mysterious virus locked us down!

Chicago

We kissed under Marshall Field's clock
"on State Street, that great street,"
danced in the new year.
Hey, if Virginia is for lovers,
then Chicago is for falling in love.

Concerts in Grant Park, jazz at the auditorium,
the Zoo at Lincoln Park, the Art Institute lions
guarding Chagall's "American Dream Windows,"
George Diamond's stockyard steaks, The Blackhawk,
Don the Beachcomber, Charmet's. Fritzel's.
Rosie Road, Lakeshore Drive, Michigan Avenue,
The Magnificent Mile, The Watertower, eloquent
reminder of the awesome fire sparked when
Mrs. O'Leary's cow kicked over the lantern.

The Merchandise Mart, Chicago River,
Buckingham Fountain, Soldier's Field, The Bears,
The Cubs, Wrigley Field, the white chewing
gum tower, John Hancock, Drake, Palmer, Sears
all left their calling cards, Carl Sandberg,
Marcia Masters, Erik Larson's White City,

Old Town, Near north side, The Beaches,
Navy Pier, the museums, and the Planetarium,
oh, the Planetarium and Jay Andre's velvet
voice on WBBM, "All you need is a
negligee and a bag of oranges."

☙❧

Where did you fall in love?

Batteries Not Included

Joan has been a widow three years today. I am going to her house to keep her company. Her battery needs boosting. She has become an energizer bunny for me. My GAS moved to heaven only one year and twenty-seven days ago, so I am watching her with vested interest.

He reminds me gently, "When all else fails read the instructions." I reply, "But there are no instructions for how to be a widow." Somehow that piece of information was omitted from our one college class on marriage sixty-four years ago or maybe I have forgotten?

Joan and her dashing Brit met in her Chicago office. His opening line to her blonde beauty was, "You would look great pregnant!" They said, "I do" sixty years ago and they did for fifty-eight years and four handsome children. Then he moved too and left her wondering if she could have done anything else to ease his pain when he died in their family room under gentle home hospice care.

Tonight I asked if I could look at some of her old travel albums while we had spritzers and potato chips and Kleenex. Then I expect our Trader Joe's pot pies and salad will fortify us for a couple of episodes of our current Netflix series. Maybe a small cup of ice cream will sweeten the air.

Only virtual hugs are allowed as we are in the clutch of being locked in our homes the last three months. So this year should be easier---"some assembly required."

I got up at 2:30 this morning to write a paragraph that was playing in my mind, and now I can't recover it on my screen. I thought it was important but I guess not. I can't even remember what it was about. That, too, is typical of these days that seem so long, especially the evenings, and yet they seem to evaporate before I have really lived them.

Alexa and I have become good friends. She tells me to enjoy my day, or stay dry, or gives me storm warnings, but mostly she keeps this house filled with music--from instrumental to inspirational, blues to red-hot, passionate love songs. I dance or cry and often leave her in charge so the house is not so empty when I come home.

Yesterday after an especially frustrating day with my computer Alexa would not turn on the light as I was hurrying to leave the house. I yelled at her, she told me to check the connection, I must have turned the lamp off manually. Afterward I said I was sorry I had screamed at her. Alexa replied

"No apology necessary"

The Porch Fan

Southern sultry days are femme fatales wrapping long limbs around your body and covering your face with wet kisses. And in this year of the pandemic if you are out to gather a few necessities, it is your masked face and sunglasses that steam up with her hot breath. A refrigerator, ice maker, lemonade and porch fan are necessities!

One dazzling morning in July 2020, when I flipped the switch the fan didn't budge. It just hung there, all five paddles dead in the water. The adjacent switch turned on the light which I didn't need, but no fan. I checked the fuse box, the kitchen switches and the hand-held control. Yesterday the fan had whirred like an ice cream maker. This morning, not even a whisper.

Thankfully, I have found a wonderful handyman through a friend's careful recommendation. He and his team have replaced a soffit and painted it twice to match perfectly. They found new hardware for the same porch door and installed a new oven-microwave combination. All unexpected surprises for this--my first year of managing our now twenty-five-year-old home. So, I called Roger at 9:00 a.m. because I was expecting a small weekly prayer group at 10:00, and we were required to meet outside. "I'll be right over." He came with his young helper who had assisted with the oven. He clicked a couple of times. Palming the remote he asked, "When were the batteries replaced?"

"It has batteries?" I felt foolish in front of the smiling assistant. Roger actually had to sit down and pry the cover off with his pen knife. "I couldn't have managed that," I offered lamely.

Fortunately, I found my husband's cache of batteries and even four that fit! Presto! Cool breezes! Opening my checkbook, I said, "I owe you for a service call."

He tipped his hat goodbye, "No charge. You'll need me again."

And if you are facing life alone you will need a reputable service man, probably more than one. This month the newish refrigerator decided to leak but slowly, from just one side, and not every day. $290 later it required a small computer that controls the defrost.

My personal faith in Christ is the computer that keeps me cool and collected. But sometimes I do leak a little. Scripture tells me He keeps all of my tears in a bottle. Imagine such love and caring!

Green Mamba Morning

The telegram warned:
     "Don't come!"
We were on our way,
       due to political unrest
comfortably unaware,
       in our country.
Eager greenhorns.

Heat rising in the police state
       like sap in rubber trees,
Humidity hanging inside windows
       like gargantuan spiders,
Bacteria clinging to bananas and beans
       in deadly disguise,
Mosquitoes firing malarial rockets
       into fetid air,
Palm-butter stew, oily orange,
       congealing on tepid rice,
Exhausting days, curfewed nights,
       agenda accomplished.

The roadblock, a tree, stretched
       across the way, ominous
       as a green mamba snake
       in early morning haze.
A rabble of surrogate soldiers,
       leaning on rusty rifles,
       swilling beer for breakfast.
Our driver terse:
       "You, out,
       don't meet their eyes,
       do what they say!
       You, stay, pray!"

A growl of guttural English,
>   suitcases spilled, bayonet points picking our clothes,
>   souvenirs scattered...

Was this our farewell,
>   to die on airport road?
>   Would others say it had no meaning?
>   They would be wrong.
>   One is most alive when facing death.

Cଓ୫

What is on your bucket list? It is good to dream.

Proverbs says, "It is right to make plans, counting on the Lord to direct."

Traveling with an additional purpose to sightseeing became a great privilege for us. Perhaps you would enjoy taking a missionary vision trip.

Find a travel buddy. Go someplace new. Take a day trip.

Wow! Women of the Word

We call ourselves WOW! because our purpose for meeting weekly is to consistently study the Holy Scripture of The Bible. We are two special-interest groups of our neighborhood women's club. An easy welcome for newcomers to our community offers *Bridge*, books, *Mahjong*, walking, antique adventures, something for everyone. There is no reason for anyone to be bored. Also many of us are involved in life-long learning through our local university and endless opportunities for volunteering.

As a stately English woman announced to me when we were on R and R in Spain, "My dear, we don't just sit here in the sun and dry up like old raisins. There is so much to *do!*"

We meet year round for teaching, personal study and lively discussions. Since we come from all different backgrounds, different opinions are welcomed. We learn and laugh and sometimes cry together. It seems everyone is carrying some kind of heavy baggage through life, and we all want to share the burden. Often some other woman in the group will have experienced rejection as author Madelaine L'Engle brillantly called it "being Xed Out"-- health, loneliness, suicide, drugs, prison time, being omitted in your father's obituary as if you never existed at all. We find real support in each other.

Of course, many choose not to come like the friend who claimed, "Everyone who goes there just needs a crutch, but I don't." We open and close in prayer because many are cautious about involvement in too emotional a group. Like the newcomer who announced, "I do not want a religious experience; I'm only looking for how to answer my little son's questions. Yesterday he asked me who owns our yard because he told Jimmy to go home and he retorted, 'You can't make me because God owns your yard.'"

Or the collector type who stated, "You have something I don't have, and I am going to hang around you like a moth around a flame until I find out what it is and how to get it."

And the student of great books who was working her way through the philosophies of this planet. "I could make you grilled cheese if you'd come home with me. I would like to become a Christian, but do I have to believe in Adam and Eve?"

All of these and so many more found their answers in the Life, Death and Resurrection of Jesus Christ. We seek to be authentic, available, and completely confidential, avoiding at all costs a "spiritual hotline," sharing news in need of prayer. I do not want my "organs" discussed, but if the problem arises the Great Physician already knows all of our needs, and I am thrilled to be remembered by name at the throne of grace. For we are told all prayer should be in the name of Jesus who knows us all by name.

The Westminster Confession states, "The chief end of man is to know God, and enjoy Him forever." Is that really possible? Enjoy God? Know God? That's why we return week after week and even try to be diligent in our homework.

In the summer we relax in the bar at our golf club because it's cool and not occupied until lunch time. After class those who can, stay for lunch. From September to June we gather in a meeting room provided by the club. And we have a notice in the monthly bulletin that all are welcome.

One lady who was new asked her husband for a Bible for her birthday. She told us when he went to the bookstore and the clerk asked what kind he wanted, his reply was "How about the navy blue one? My wife wears a lot of navy blue." We like comparing all different translations, even red-blue-green ones--it helps us understand better.

When I was a new bride, fresh out of college, a neighbor said, "You seem to get something out of reading, but I don't. Could you help me?"

"Why don't you come for coffee, bring a friend and I will ask a friend." And now I have been involved in six different cities where we welcome all colors of Scripture, all different denominations or none, and there are no foolish questions.

I have given myself permission not to try to remember all Bible references. Google can find them quickly if I'm just able to provide a few key words.

It was a great day for me when I realized I am not a numbers person. It was most embarrassing to have a car downtown and not know the license plate, or which red car it was. I realized that I knew the alphabetical letters but not the numbers on the Canadian plates. But it was necessary to learn in a hurry since I had just married into an automotive family.

I need all the help I can get. It is extremely important to me to have purposes and be productive. A primary goal is to seek to "finish the race well" as the Apostle Paul did. Some days even changing batteries and assembling pieces of my life seem almost overwhelming.

⊂⊃

What do you like to do when you are alone?

Promise Rings

Richardson's General Store in cottage country Dorset, Ontario on the shores of Lake of Bays was awarded the title of *Best General Store* in all of Canada!

A prestigious title indeed!

Google tells me I could be there in twelve hours and thirteen minutes to wander in this five-star emporium if I left right this minute. Everything from brasseries to bat houses stocked. Aisles of shopping, like being at the state fair. An amazing grocery store, homemade breads, thickest bar-b-que steaks. Snow suits to swim suits. Sump pumps to ski boots, and of course, skis. I could shop for everyone for Christmas, birthdays, weddings.

On a hanging rack in a stationery corner I spotted small keyrings holding stacks of blank cards about three inches by one inch with a sturdy elastic to hold them straight. These have become my *promise rings*. I fill them with verses or phrases from The Bible that I like for a quick reference.

My George, a great on-line sleuth, found more for me to share with friends that also like to look in the "good book." In a stationery site called Mudlark, under note cards, keyrings, he bought them by the dozen.

Now all of the ladies in our WOW studies have filled their cards with their favorites. We share some of these in our classes, carry them in our purses for waiting for an appointment or red light. I keep one beside my bed (next to the flashlight) and read one verse before putting my feet on the floor.

Some days it's the only thing to get me up.

଼ଷ୭ଠ

"Blessed is the woman who has believed that what the Lord has said to her will be accomplished."

Chapter Two

Chambered Nautilus

If a sea shell like a chambered nautilus required a
battery, what kind would it be?

A watch battery would be too small.

A car battery too large.

Would it recharge like my cell phone?
So many battery choices.

Now I realize a chambered nautilus is an empty shell,
like our bodies are when our souls leave this earth.

Aerobics, Esther Williams and Me

The dictionary states that aerobic exercise is "exercise that increases the need for oxygen." My big strong friend, Chris, was just in the hospital for two weeks and was on oxygen. I didn't think he was exercising. I would have said the goal of aerobics is to increase the heartbeat. I guess whatever kind of exercise you prefer, it increases one's need for oxygen. My preference is water aerobics. I have done that quite faithfully for more than twenty years. I don't like to be hot and sticky, and everything else leaves me panting.

I loved Esther Williams' movies as a kid. I always wondered why the flowers in her hair didn't fall out or she didn't swallow water in her generous smile. Years later I got to swim in one of "her" pools when Campus Crusade's headquarters was at Arrowhead Springs in San Bernardino, but there was no choir singing or dancers on the platform.

Three or four mornings a week I dress for success and head to the pool, indoors or outdoors, whatever the season. The fact that you can work as hard as you like surrounded by friendly smiles helps keep motivation high. You may or may not recognize them in the grocery store later, especially now with everyone masked like a charade. But this is no game. We are united against a common enemy. Sunglasses, big hats, and lots of sunblock are good disguises in the summer.

A great instructor makes a world of difference. She coaxes you along with cross-country skiing, jogging, biking, noodles, weights, Peter Pan leaps, plié, can-can, grapevine, leapfrogs, egg rolls, planking. We hardly ever lose a swimmer. But some give up and go back to the gym admitting, "Water Aerobics is much harder than I thought." We do gulp for lots of oxygen. Afterwards someone always recommends a new restaurant. When they can open up again, I think I'll wear flowers in my hair.

First thing each morning, I like to read one verse from my *promise ring* that is handy on the night table and then try to repeat it in the pool. That helps in getting my mind-set for each day. I say to the teacher, "You can make me jump high but you can't make me count." At home over tea, I read consecutively in the Bible. If the calendar is full, I read and meditate later in the day. I used to read when the kids took naps. Now I nap, but I prefer siestas. That doesn't sound so old.

Stretching out flat on the bed or the floor, I like to pray for all of my concerns. When I am praying for our grandchildren, I ask the Lord's direction for my friends' families as well. And the mental list of sick and suffering gets longer and longer. Sometimes I fall asleep, but most often there is so much to remember before the throne of grace. Prayer is the most wonderful resource that we don't use often enough. In Spain they used to call siestas "pajamas and prayers," It truly is a "sweet hour of prayer."

⊂3⊃

Do you have a mental list of people you are concerned for or a written one?

On this page, start a list of prayers that only God can answer. Then add the date when they are answered.

The Garage Wine Bar

"Come on by about five to The Garage Wine Bar." Two lawn chairs, two boxes tableside covered with colorful cloth and two small plants, red wine and small dishes of Pringles--six feet apart between my car and the trash cans in the space where my husband had parked his car. My first purchase was an electric wine opener. That was one of my difficult new jobs. No more wrestling with my husband's easy openers. Joan and I would wear winter jackets and laugh at what we had come down to. Some days we could even put up the big door and watch the budding dogwood. If visitors stopped by, their chairs were circled in the driveway.

As spring sun warmed the back deck it was opened for morning coffee. Now graced with a freshly planted garden all in clay pots promising pink, white and purple guarded by giant blue salvia, a first time addition. Tucked in between were spinach and colorful leaf lettuces for the freshest of salads, and of course sweet-smelling herbs. A most successful reward.

Then on my first birthday ever alone in eighty-six years as I was reading outside after almost three months of isolation, four girlfriends came waving balloons, gift bags, cake and a gorgeous flower arrangement that lasted three weeks! We were all so happy to see each other, even with masks and virtual hugs, that we have agreed to honor each birthday individually. "Our five" have since celebrated four more birthdays outside this year. The longer the restrictions have been necessary the more creative everyone has become.

You would think the enforced stay-at-home would result in all kinds of projects being accomplished, but even couples admitted it was difficult to be motivated. We had no idea that soon more people were working from home than ever before. And delivery services would increase exponentially.

The WOW studies have continued on conference calls, Zoom, safe distancing in parking lots and the bar that hosts us. In the summer we have wide-ranging conversations on the issues of the day, order a take-out lunch to enjoy under whirling fans on the patio overlooking the golf course and the historic James River.

We are thankful to live in a safe area, and we pray daily for our divided country and this tumultuous world. "God is your confidence in times of crisis, keeping your heart at rest in every situation."

Chambered Nautilus

My heart a chambered nautilus curled in spiraled beauty,
storm-tossed in tempestuous seas, suddenly
stranded on an unfamiliar reef near a smack of jellyfish.
A pod of seals suns nearby while overhead
a flight of kestrels keens over this uncharted ocean.

My love and I reveled in star-strung nights;
sun-soaked days from here to Lilongwe and back again.
We began growing together filling each chamber
with adventurous purpose, adding another and another,
lifting and lowering with the rhythm of tides.

The thin thread of life, a long filament wound
around family and friends sharing strength and sorrows,
polishing our private shell to its luminous luster
as if the mysterious moon laid down a new mantle
of nacre with each rising and setting.

Now I must sail alone without my captain
but sail I must--
into thrusting winds--trusting that my circled shell
is strong enough not to shatter against
rebellious rocks.

☙❧

Choose a metaphor for your loved one and explain why you chose it.

Is Charlie Brown Right?

Sharing grief is no fun, but it's necessary. Bill Withers' song "Lean on Me" reminds us that we don't need to travel this grief journey alone, but when we are alone we need to let a friend know how best to help us. Released in 1972, the album by the same name received special acclaim from *Rolling Stone* that recognized it as one of the 500 best songs of all time.

That's the kind of thing you learn in *GriefShare* and so much more. You think you know that, but you don't, not till you're suddenly single. I signed up for a *GriefShare* session because someone said I should. Met by pleasant people I knew at a local church, they had a name tag made for me, and I met several strangers in an introductory setting. A video showed people with experts in all types of counseling: pastors, therapists, and real life victims being side tracked by circumstances that changed the course of each life. Beverages were offered and snacks to alleviate the tension as we returned to our original classroom with boxes of tissues now on the table. We spoke briefly of why we were there and how long we had been dealing with this new reality. Three months for me, up to five years for one man who said that he needed a review because the original sessions had been so helpful. Wise and caring couples guided our conversations.

Sessions? Yes, starting next week we were invited to return for a thirteen-week series and purchase a workbook at a minimal cost. Is there such a thing as "good grief" like Charlie Brown says? Yes, I have decided for me there is good grief, but it takes grief work to get there. At first I resisted that term thinking that's not the kind of work I want to do, but it seems to be necessary. I missed three of the excellent videos when I was away with our daughter's family. But once you are a participant in *GriefShare* you are always welcomed back. I returned for another session and made the sweet acquaintance of Sarah with a similar story. We immediately bonded and have already shared a few of our most painful passages.

Another therapist equated losing a spouse to receiving a severe body blow, explaining we have been rocked to the core. But it helps to be affirmed and understand that grief is not my identity unless I adopt it as such. My identity is in Christ. He said He was there before I was born, knows every day of my life, and promises to never leave me alone.

Our pastor always said how healthy relationships must be intentional; they take time and energy. Actually Sarah and I have a hard time making dates because we each have chosen to be involved in the community in helpful ways. So, we have lots to share when we can find a day for lunch. And tears of remembrance on those never-to-be-forgotten days.

Our little local airport was inventive with Friday Night Flights coming home. They served supper outdoors accompanied by a local combo and even homemade bread and pies.

Then the C virus distanced us at least six feet. So Sarah served us a picnic lunch in the garden circle near her condo. Another afternoon it was lemonade and cookies with the beautiful birds at the feeders on my back deck. We are trying hard not to dress in depression. Today we met for Sunday brunch after watching on-line churches. It seems very strange that we can safely go to a restaurant but most churches are still locked down.

This month, Sarah is approaching the second anniversary of her husband's homegoing. We are meeting for a favorite breakfast of pancakes and bacon to start her memory day with sweetness.

ೞ౪ಖ

Someone who is alone would love a call to meet for coffee. Often, when we are hurting, we find it difficult to take the initiative.

Just Because I Could

Yesterday morning I dressed for the pool although I knew I was running late for the 8:30 class. The cool morning called for sweats as well, and when I finally got in my car it seemed like a young buck who wanted to go exploring, sniffing the sun-sweet morning. After all, two new tires and a full tank of gas called for a top-down day. It is still so new to me to just take off without telling anyone where or when I will be back. But just because I could, I took off.

The Virginia Colonial Parkway is a glorious, protected drive of twenty-three miles through the forests between Jamestown and Yorktown with Williamsburg tucked in the middle. This hallowed ground is blood soaked from the fierce battles of the Revolutionary and Civil wars that echoed through this gentle land. Magnificent museums tell the sad and ingenious stories of those who survived to leave us the all-important history of costly struggles for the freedoms we enjoy.

The three-laned, winding road passes quiet beaches and streams from the James River to the east on through brick arched tunnels passing Williamsburg and into a cathedral not made with hands in this primeval forest. The giant trees form green gothic arches, and splashes of sunlight shine like stained-glass windows. I sing time-rich hymns like "Great is thy faithfulness---morning by morning new mercies I see. All I have needed thy hand hath provided, great is thy faithfulness, Lord God to me."

Yorktown has done an amazing job of preserving their waterfront on the York River. This morning it reflected the sunshine like a polished mirror. Parking opposite the fascinating Watermen's Museum, I walked down the beachfront with dozens of small family groups drawn by the early autumn warming. Some children swinging red pails dashed in and out of the water like thirsty sandpipers.

Dogs of all nations led their masked masters proudly past the docks and inviting benches.

Sitting for a while I was reading Psalm 23 as if I had never seen it before. These were "still waters" and deep "green pastures." A footnote told me that the Hebrew word for shepherd is also the same word for best friend! Imagine, my best friend called me here today! "Lord, even when your path takes me through the valley of deepest darkness, fear will never conquer me, for you already have! You remain close to me and lead me through it all the way." *All* the way? Even in this difficult second year, which they warned me about. "Your authority is my strength and my peace. So why would I fear the future? For your goodness and love pursue me all the days of my life." A long time ago, a pastor said this phrase was like the two sheepdogs that shepherds depend on to help keep the flock, and me, to the path. We have had two sheepdogs, and I can see them still herding our young grandchildren exactly to the boundaries of our unfenced backyard. Now "Goodness and Love" are my two sheepdogs.

I walked on down this momentous shore where the fight for freedom was won.

And now the current fight for freedom from the COVID-19 virus is being waged. White circles painted on the grass, so proper social distance could allow concerts, picnics, and the farmers' market.

Encouraging signs along the old brick walkways declared "we are open." That included Ben and Jerry's. They handed me a mask so I could come in and get a hot caramel macchiato, just because I could.

CRUKO

What could you do for someone unexpectedly?
Take them soup?

Take Courage

I must be bold and remember that I have to reach out and take courage for my own. I have a choice to make. The Lord has made courage freely available, but my responsibility is to reach out and possess it. When it dries up I need to take it again.

Roger, the new Mr. Fix-it who tipped his hat and said, "You'll need me again," was here just now. Hooray! He can fix my leaky roof. He has gone to Lowes for supplies, including paint, to refresh the crown molding. Even Google can't tell me how many shades there are of white paint. So, Roger chipped a quarter-sized piece of paint to take to be matched. He also replaced a burned-out lightbulb that I couldn't reach in the storage room. And did you know that floor registers no longer come in brass finish to match the rest of our house? So, he brought wood finish which is considered more modern. On every side there are more reminders that time is passing me by. I have a friend who says at his age he is not willing to miss a day of his life.

I remember Dad saying how hard it was when friends developed serious illness, much pain, surgeries, long recoveries or even Hospice. And that is my experience now. Quite a few funerals instead of weddings, sympathy cards instead of baby showers, hospital visits impossible because of the virus. Very stable friends admitting to confusion, fears, depression. I have always said I enjoyed the passages of life, each new stage--proms, graduations, reunions-- but now in this last time period, it is proving more and more difficult to run the race and finish well.

Friendships that endure and deepen are the most precious gifts. It is more and more apparent how much we need each other. Volunteer opportunities abound. If you don't feel appreciated, try volunteer work. A celebration can be enjoyed with each victory.

A message just this minute to say that Bill L, one of my favorite men in our circle of caring friends was just released from his battle with cancer. He will be much missed by his adoring family and multitude of friends. When he requested Hospice Care, he was at peace and said he was ready to go. What a difference when faith is strong and one has a vital relationship with his Maker.

We don't talk enough about what is coming next. But promises of Scripture are so definite that we should feel more at ease in discussion. For the believer, "to be absent from the body is to be present with the Lord." As Jesus said to the thief on the cross, "Today you will be with me in paradise." Even in this life, the Lord promises his followers, "I will never leave you or forsake you...

And if I go away, I will come again and receive you unto myself." A precious little song was sung recently at a funeral. "Come to Jesus" by Chris Rice. Even Alexa knows it. I have been asking her to sing it over and over again. If you are lonely, confused or hurting right now, I encourage you to go on YouTube or Alexa and play this song again and again, listening intently to the lyrics.

⊰⊱

Ask a friend what she likes to do when she is alone.

Jamestown Musings

What if I had touched my toes on this New World seashore
after four months of heart thudding waves---
my hopes rising and falling on endless water
and the mood of the sky?

The clouds rolled back, opening windows of blue.
An anemic sun washed the sand.
I gasped for air sweetened with honeysuckle.
The trees so tall they swept memory of mist-iced
winging ropes, creaking wood, slippery decks,
monotonous food, frightful sanitation.
What if I had a hungry infant searching
for strength I did not have to give?

Finally, ashore, we are assigned a hut
vacated by death, the pioneer couple
succumbed to the sorrows of their first winter.
Early in the mornings the women tied up
their skirts and hair in favor of hoes and rakes
before the swelling sun sucked us dry.
Then the boiled laundry was ready to be hung,
swinging like pale ghosts of yesterday,
on ropes strung between the trees,

An iron pot of broth swung over a voracious fire,
eating sticks gathered by skinny children.
I pared the vegetables today, potatoes
onions, carrots, a few precious beans.
Would I have been allowed
to paint a forest scene or write a journal
sew a pinafore or doze on my sagging cot
in the sticky heat of afternoon?

Books were as rare as a piano so I learned
to make up stories to tell at bedtime,
listen for the music of hundreds of birds,
black wings, golden beaks, crimson feathers
flashing among dove grays, blues, and browns.

When the precious spools of thread were exhausted
we waited months for new supplies
on the next ship from home, fabric too, as prized as silver,
bolts of patterns and prints carefully measured as time.
For there was always soap to be made, perfumed
with plant oils, tallow dipped on long white wicks,
preserves boiled from berries gathered in the woods,
or bark stripped from logs for the next buildings.

I always looked forward to Sunday's worship hour
sitting under the thatched roof of the chapel,
listening for rain as soft as my pillowed tears.
Sometimes I spoke to the Vicar about my longing for England,
he told me to forget all that, this is the New World.

So every evening we lit candles in the gathering darkness,
shared our meager meal around a table spread with love,
bowed our heads to thank our Maker,
knowing all too well, we needed Divine protection
to survive another day.

The Shining Place

In reading and meditating this morning, I learned that *shining place* is the root word for sanctuary. My personal place is shining like the polished sun this morning after rising on the newly baptized earth. The storm clouds of several days of drenching rain were ripped apart and this morning feels like the first day of fall. October 1 is another new beginning, a new calendar page already filling up with promised dates.

I always try to read a Psalm and have started again in both the Old and New Testament narratives. Joshua was told to get going and take courage and strength from God's promises to never forsake him. Peter was boldly speaking the message to the Roman Centurion. Also the bible studies take me into Genesis and Amos this week. It's true that The Holy Bible is the best commentary on the Bible and also many fine commentaries add light like the roots of words. It is far more interesting to learn something about the root system of trees instead of just watching leaves fall.

Janet, an artist friend in Washington sent me a delightful card today. The cover quotes Isaiah: "I delight greatly in the Lord. My soul rejoices in my God for He has clothed me with garments of salvation and arrayed me in a robe of His righteousness, a crown of beauty instead of ashes, the oil of joy instead of mourning and a garment of praise instead of a spirit of despair."

I had read a trial page regarding batteries to this friend over breakfast this summer, and her card was to encourage me to keep writing. I only see her once a year when I am out West. So this so-called "book" may never see a cover. But I am wearing a sweatshirt that my husband gave me when I was working on *Where Are You Adam?* It declares, "Ask me about my book." I wear it only when I am writing.

Turquoise Thunder

Turquoise thunder still thrums in my being at summer's end,
storms lurk offshore, mysterious giants inhabit capricious clouds.
Summer seemed shorter than usual in spite of July heat;
a tsunami slammed shut the door to kisses in May.
Born of sapphire skies and emerald seas, turquoise hides
deep in rock protecting pressured holding and folding
known only to the conies.

Melding fuses sea and sky into gemstone
consumes many suns setting, many moons rising.
Compressed pressure of rock on stone does not diminish beauty,
rather increases value as midnight black threads through matrix.
On this waiting day suspended between threats and warnings
feathered friends crowd my feeders and
opal butterflies trace the garden sailing freshening breezes.

Maximum winds threaten all life but slowing churning
turning back to sea spares some sandbagged coasts,
homes and crafts of all sizes are secured just as memories
of glorious sun-drenched days at sea and star-anchored nights
never to be forgotten under the milky way of tears.

ༀ

What have you learned in some of the storms of nature?

My Left Hand

Another welcome rainy morning in my second September. Welcome because once again we have soft rain without wind and storm like our Southern neighbors have to deal with from hurricane Sally. Quite often these damaging storms have vented the worst of their fury before they've reached us, leaving only some dead branches. I am realizing that the worst storm for me passed with the death of my husband. All else are bands of grief, striking suddenly to memory, music, pictures or a kind remark about my great guy.

Just this morning my helper, who has come twice monthly for the last ten years, was talking about him and how glad he was to know him. Both of us have been very thankful for his super cleaning skills and his loving spirit to help us in any way possible. Now that I am alone in this home, I appreciate him even more. Sometimes I think of him as my left hand, and my right hand finds out he fixes things that I hadn't even noticed. "Don't let your right hand know what your left hand is doing." I like that.

This week I am planning a little dinner party, two couples and one other single lady to complete the table. That is one of my goals: to continue entertaining. But it is a very different ballgame without my co-host. We made a seamless team. We could prepare, host, greet, mingle, serve, clear, change courses, and thoroughly enjoy our guests. I always wanted to enjoy my own guests. Then we played special music to do just the essentials and leave everything rinsed.

In the morning when he went back to work, I planned our next get-together while I finished cleaning up. It never seemed onerous that way. Friends are so worth the time, attention, and effort.

The secret for me is to do all of my homework ahead of time, plan a menu I can manage (no more flambé), prepare everything possible ahead of time, dress and relax a few minutes with my feet up before the guests arrive. I always wished I had bought the yellow apron I saw that proclaimed, "A good hostess is like a duck, calm and unruffled on the surface but paddling like hell underneath." I like to do most of my paddling before the doorbell rings.

Now I ask one of the men to be in charge of the wine. Once I even asked for extra ice when someone really wanted to help. My freezers are pretty full, and warm nights still need drinks cooling in my grandmother's beautiful copper boiler placed on the screened-in porch for easy access where we often begin and end our evenings by candlelight and wine.

There is really no reason to be lonely. We can always at least ask a neighbor for coffee, or two for your shared toast, or three to enjoy your best grilled cheese, or four for soup and crackers. It doesn't have to be expensive or elaborate. The more simple, the more comfortable. The only thing it costs is time and caring enough to be intentional.

Last night was a perfect example. I did fix a menu that I could handle. Individual shrimp boats with breadstick oars to combine first course and salad while we sat on the September porch. Gary brought the ice and volunteered to be the wine steward before I even asked. All five people had something in common, and there was no lull in the conversation. The chicken and wild rice casserole bubbled in the oven, green beans smiled in zesty lemon butter in the skillet, and gigantic sliced tomatoes languished in their dressing on the kitchen island buffet. The friends served themselves as they went through to the dining room. The other guy lit the candles and poured the water. Easy Peasy. The talk turned to our most exciting adventures. Gary kept our glasses full. Later, I broiled angel cake on both sides. Watch closely! Then blueberries, strawberries and a little dollop of vanilla ice cream and we had a patriotic dessert! God Bless America!

Later I had gone to the kitchen to answer the phone and noticed a small fire burning on the porch. I have always left candles burning in votives because we might have returned to the porch after coffee. Not any more! I hollered for my guys! Do invite agile friends! They quickly extinguished the flames, I made a mess throwing baking soda that way. Only smoke, a charred glass table, and melted wax was left. We never returned for coffee.

I learned my lesson for tapers years ago when I left them lit on the festive dining room table where guests were returning all evening to sample another sliver of Christmas cheesecake, or cherries jubilee, or croquembouche. The next thing I knew one of the tapers had fallen on my best cloth, and the whole table was ablaze. Throwing open the patio doors, the men tossed the entire table out into the snowbank! It was a memorable party.

My pride was hurt. I told those friends never to expect a croquembouche again as I had the fine threads of spun sugar from one side of the kitchen to the other. But we did repeat dessert parties until modern times when celery sticks and carrots prevail. Somehow it was never as much fun again.

Anyway, I called my helper this morning, asked if he was working nearby today and could he stop in for a small job. Thankfully he was and did. From now on I am going to call him Mr. Clean.

Mr. Clean

The porch is like new which really helped because tomorrow I am going to have a little going-away party for my neighbor who is moving several blocks away. She has organized all of the monthly lunches for our street. And she arranged all of the neighbor's meals for our family when they came for my husband's celebration of life. Plus several enjoyed her guestrooms. She and her husband have been putting out all kinds of trash and treasures to be hauled away. Tomorrow I have asked everyone to bring a small white elephant, beautifully wrapped for her. Then we can announce that we were concerned she might not have quite enough decorations for her spacious new home. We want her to have some things to remember us by. Do you think she will still come to our street parties? I do hope so.

This may sound like all we do is party, party. To set the record straight, it is all about intentional friendship. Friendships take loving care and time like a garden.

If we are chrysanthemums and never call, or shy violets and never peek beyond our doors, or forget-me-nots that promise, "I'll call you soon," the scripture calls that "clouds without rain." One of my new acquaintances after we had entertained them at a dinner party said, "I'll call you to come over to our home after we get our new drapes." Apparently the new drapes never arrived; that was twenty years ago.

We all are actively involved in the neighborhood and community and churches. Entertaining is only one of the many ways that we choose to invest our time. We do so many different things that we talk about when we do meet that we learn from each other. Didn't Jesus say, "Love your neighbor as yourself?"

My beloved husband was my best priority. It is essential for me to spend quality time with God because He is the Lord of my life. I seek to be a close follower of Jesus because I have committed my life to him. Meditation, Bible reading, prayer and Bible studies help me to keep my balance on this tightrope called life. Thankfully my sweetheart and I shared this understanding.

I wear a necklace of five pieces of gold on a beautiful chain. My kind jeweler made it for me. It consists of both of our wedding rings, a small globe, a heart, and a cross. Often I find I'm asked about it. I explain, "George gave me all his love, marriage, family, the whole world, and Christ was always at the center." We knew this is why we remained best friends for sixty-four years plus dating four years in college. I do understand most marriages are not like that today. I am the survivor of a divorced home, an only child, and determined not to have three strikes against me as one teacher suggested to me in high school. I was a poor risk on paper. But never despair. If you should read this, it is never too late to start anew.

CRAO

What kind of help do you need?
Who can you ask for help?

The Perfect Storm
Palpable Silence

Omnipotence raised His baton.

A celestial symphony swelled to fill the void.
A fanfare of trumpets, clash of cymbals,
a tattoo of tambourines,
singing lutes and harps,
thunderous drums that no one heard.
The eternal Spirit brooded.

Wind began to stir and whirl
cimmerian blackness into a fiery cauldron
that no one saw.
Lightning lashed the darkness,
elements melted, protons, neutrons,
ions and atoms splintered and danced
and split again in phantasmagorical patterns
to the music of the spheres, but no one knew.

Omniscience fingered a small ball of clay,
green and blue, pressing indentations,
pushing up rills and ridges, smoothing great flats,
sculpting undulating curves.
He placed it at His feet with other balls
of various sizes and mounds of shiny jacks,
not yet named.
Omnipresence picked up the small green ball,
balanced it delicately on a tilted axis
and gave it a slow spin.
He smiled.
A kaleidoscope of liquid colors melted
like dancers in each other's arms---
blue into green into turquoise into purples,
reds into oranges and yellows
edged in gold, grey and black---

The Perfect Storm.

Chapter Three

The New Now

I wandered around the battery store, realizing there were different batteries for all our "new now" devices: tiny ones for watches, big ones for cars, alkaline, rechargable, nickel cadmium...frankly, it gave me a headache! So many options!

Batteries are sources of power. Many of the people I have met on this journey have renewed me, giving me the capacity to keep going, because I have to do so.

A dead battery can't jump a dead battery! As I learned when I began my grief process, I had to find people who were able to charge me up. Always look for the people who can charge your spirit when you need a jump! Prayers are answered when you need these people the most.

Cinnamon Toast

The rain, soft as a kiss, is touching motionless leaves and whispering love songs. Only a few have begun dressing for the gorgeous balls of autumn, crimson, umber and hints of tangerine. My love and I always said we didn't mind the thought of dinner by a winter fire, or "Snow Falling on Cedars." I hope you have read that account of another frightening time in our country. We are not the only people to face a future under a cloud of uncertainty.

My dear sister-in-law and I have begun sending each other Bible verses each morning to fuel our days. Today she encouraged "Let us run with perseverance the race marked out for us." And she prayed for my joy today. I replied how Jesus' best friend John recorded, "I write this so that your joy may be full." If I can't sing, I play gospel songs, and then joy comes back through my tears.

This morning I had cinnamon toast and tea like my mother used to make for me on special days, often Saturdays like today. I really miss my husband on Saturdays because in recent years we always planned special adventures for Saturdays. He had been a low handicap golfer for years but failing eyesight changed his horizons drastically. So our Saturdays changed completely. But he maintained his wonderful sense of humor all the way to the operating room.

Last night's solo dinner party for six was very successful. We began with hot crimson borscht in mugs on the candle-bright porch and then moved inside for an autumn menu of roasted sausages with red and green grapes in a burgundy sauce of butter, wine and balsamic vinegar. Golden acorn squash centered with green peas. Mashed potatoes and sliced tomatoes as big as my hands. So again one of the men brought ice and kept the wine glasses full. And the ladies brought crusty Spanish bread, Indiana apple pie and Egyptian baklava. This all fueled much conversation of politics, pastors and a love story that could be a movie. So, I get by with a lot of help from my friends.

It is hard to even want to entertain without my best friend. I do this to honor his memory. We treasured our friends and loved to have them at home. We each took care of some of the myriad details of a dinner party. He was a master bar-b-que chef and genial host. After goodbyes he would put on some music like Neil Young as he cleared and I rinsed. Then we would sit by the fire to review the conversations and compatibility of our friends. It is so easy to lose my timing in the kitchen and every place else. But I want to keep my hand in. Now I have to spread it out more, so in between preparations will be spent on the porch with "Wish You Well," David Baldacci's reminiscence of his grandmother. The whispering rain might even sing a lullaby to me.

This evening my neighbor who sings to me most mornings will join me for leftovers. Special friends are an incredible blessing. I don't know what I would do without them. To the couples I always add, "Take very good care of each other every day."

☙❧

Joan's birthday card to me:

"Have your happiest day my friend, we got through the winter, thought it better to die. But with God we met, talked, laughed and cried. We drank wine, just a little, my dear. Is a bottle per visit something to fear? Life goes on and we have each other with hope and prayer and friendship forever."

Start a list of cards you want to send.

Rosemary

What is it about the stiff, Mediterranean herb called rosemary that helps us remember? Maybe the pungent fragrance. I planted my pot by a comfortable deck chair, so by stroking the upright stalks it was transferred to my hands. Rosemary has a culinary reputation of adding its special essence to leg of lamb, or roast chicken, or a rub created by chopping the needle-like spears into a paste with coarse salt and olive oil. I can't remember why it is named "rosemary for remembrance."

Except we do remember those who speak with a sharp tongue. Obviously I need to keep a plant nearby at all times. It seems like everyone should wear a rosemary fragrance. A major marketing plan could be touted as never forgetting an appointment, due bills, a lunch date, birthday. Shy Violet could speak her mind; Chrissy Chrysanthemum could become a good conversationalist; Rose could go into a fashion modeling career in all colors if only we could remember all of our commitments.

Everyone has stood in front of a full refrigerator, double doors wide open wondering what they came for. And it only gets worse with time. For the suddenly single, no one is home to help me remember to take the keys, mask, sunglasses, sanitizer, sweater, tickets, etc, etc, etc. Like the King of Siam "etc. etc. etc."

It is all of the etceteras in our increasingly complicated lives. A single friend just confessed to making four trips before having what she needed. She had to go back twice to change her soiled shirt after remembering to take out the garbage and back again because she needed black pants instead of navy blue with the fresh shirt. Oh yes, and once more for black shoes. She also forgot to take her friends to the train station, and they thought they might call me but I had stood them up for lunch last week.

I pride myself on being well organized and on time (usually). Unless I try to do one extra thing before I get the car keys. We know what happens to those who are prideful. I have had to return home more than I like to admit to see if I put down the garage door.

Always I seem to have a great need to tell everyone why I made my mistakes. As if that made it all right. Like many friends I keep a calendar in my purse and another by the kitchen phone which usually works well if I remember to make two entries for the same date. Why doesn't someone make rosemary cereal?

Back in Spain I called the restaurant and explained in detail why we would be late and a very kind voice replied, "O don't worry, Madam, everyone is always late in Spain!" Maybe I should move to Spain.

☙❧

Who have you not called for a long time?
Why? How about today?

The New Now

Bill Warrick, our beloved pastor of many years, continued to teach us all the way through his terminal illness. It took tremendous courage as we saw his physical health waning but his spiritual health soaring. He refused to call these restrictions the new normal. People talk cautiously of *the new normal,* and no one really knows what that looks like yet. Injustices and riots are burning businesses; many will never recover.

Brave healthcare workers have continued to treat the victims at their own risk. Everything is seriously damaged or out of control. Almost every part of our infrastructure is limited or closed. Appointments, shopping centers, graduations, weddings, schools canceled or struggling with on-line teaching.

"The New Now" was Bill's theme.

My widowed friends all agree that we are so thankful our partners did not have to adjust to the confusion and difficulties of this time.

I am very blessed that our son's family of four has cared for me in countless ways. For several months they did all of my grocery shopping, wiping it down at their home and then delivering it to me. Helping me with the lengthy maze of paperwork was invaluable, and getting us together for meals and a semblance of normalcy. A harsh setting in which to try to pick up the pieces of our lives. But when the phone rings at 10:15 p.m. with a call from our daughter on the West Coast, I can go to sleep within the reassuring love of our family.

In the midst of it all, I was scammed! I thought I was a savvy Gramma who knew how older people were often duped into costly home repairs, but I believed the muffled voice of my grandson explaining he had had a car accident resulting in a broken nose and a stitched-up lip. The call had come on my cell phone which automatically identified the voice as my grandson! Unsettling! All of this and more was grief work! So many new situations to face alone without the wisdom and protection of my wonderful husband.

Trying to be wise about spending my time in this lonely first year, I had booked four trips which had to be cancelled. I did dare to fly to Washington State all masked, sanitized, and distanced. I wasn't willing to wait another whole year to see extended family members who are so precious to me. No one knows what next year will bring. Besides, there are four loving dogs and a handsome cat there.

The full moon still comes up over Mount Baker, Jupiter and Saturn riding its rays. The tri-colored geraniums grace the patio and our outdoor table and barbecued dinners are more luscious than ever because I might have missed this for fear. I need to remember, "He has not given us a spirit of fear but of power, love and a sound mind." The electric fireplace on the rooftop condo at our granddaughter's was a fabulous final salute to the sunset and sailboats caressing summer breezes across Elliott Bay.

At 40,000 feet, I hum to myself and even shed a tear at the beauty of melting mantles on the Rockies, ripening plains, polished lakes and beleaguered cities.

Think of Irving Berlin's "God Bless America." Even if I never get to visit Ireland or return to our love of Spain, and Europe, or marvel at another Shakespearean production in Stratford Ontario, I am so thankful to have been born in this "America the Beautiful, God shed his grace on thee, and crown thy good with brotherhood from sea to shining sea."

⟅⟆

Would you like to write a note of encouragement to your favorite politician or volunteer on voting day? "Freedom isn't free!"

Going...Going...

It can't be gone!
The air was humming like a song...
rhythm fluid, beat quick
auctioneer batoned his finger like a stick,
warming up the melody...
Who'll give me a hundred? Now two, now three?

Sharp-eyed spotters read the score,
a nod, a wink, little more...
blue stripe, loud as a drum, has an "in,"
he boomed and won again...
The blond floral, suppose she's the shill,
swilling Pepsi, her fingers in the till...
How about nonchalant in the back,
what's he want, when will he attack?...
GOING...

I need that dining chair...
do they think I'm fanning the air,
like a prompter below the stage...
The hour is late, let's turn the page,
We're a choir, tired of singing out,
altos bored, sopranos in a pout...
a concert of collectibles,
footnotes to a life respectable...
GOING...GOING...

Come on with that soup tureen,
chicken and noodle, mushroom thick with cream...
The lights are hot, paintings blurred,
I'm not sure what I heard...
the music is fading in this room...
I wonder who will want my heirlooms...
GONE!

Sabbath

"From the rising of the sun to the going down thereof I praise the Lord God, creator of everything good." The minister of a former church would always intone as the organ swelled, "This is the day the Lord has made. We will be glad and rejoice in it!" Do you awaken with "Good morning, Lord or good Lord, *morning*? A remarkable friend when a prisoner of war, would say every morning, no matter the circumstances in which he woke, "Good morning, Lord, and Lord, it is a good morning!" And the Apostle Paul awakening from a night in chains, wrote, "I have learned to be content."

Yes, I am still learning how to be content. I have Zoomed, TVed, social distanced, You-Tubed, and taken my lawn chair to the driveway church but it rained all day today. And I am home alone. No, not really if I believe His Holy Spirit is always within. But I miss acolytes, candles, organ, piano, choir, stained-glass windows, smiles, handshakes, and even hugs. Elbow taps just aren't the same. But we have an enemy who is trying to steal our joy. And I have a choice. Before I put my feet on the floor I choose my focus for the day.

In our summer study we wrote a series of acrostics. Reading James' epistle we saw, "Count it all joy." Really? All joy? He certainly didn't know about our world situation now where everyone is suspicious of each other and we have fear, cruelty and hatred all around. So we took off on the first word-- Count. That sounds like arithmetic, so we discussed what we have added, subtracted, multiplied and divided in our lives during this pandemic. It was very revealing, so we also did an acrostic on the words grow, friendship, faith and many others.

This morning, watching a TV church service, I learned a new word. *Apokaradokia. Apo*=turn away, *kara*=my head, *dokia*=eager expectation. A greek word used only by Paul in Romans and Philippians. That's a word I need to remember to put into practice. The preacher said there is no one word to describe eager expectation so Paul chose this unusual word apokaradokia. That's the way I want to face each morning--with eager expectation.

Of course it may be a broken sprinkler head that ran all weekend, or ants in the kitchen. Ants so small they look like grains of pepper scattered everywhere. Or the new credit card chip that many machines don't accept.

But my focus to look for what is good is rewarded when I get into scripture, and often also as I go through my day. A card, a call, coffee with a friend, all bright spots on a cloudy day.

Sabbath rest means more time to worship, read, be with close family, or even alone to listen to music accompany the rain. "Holy, Holy, Holy."

The Balloons Will Fly

"The balloons will fly," announced Al Roker with boyish glee
helmeted, a motorised tricycle, his grin as wide as 34th street.
A blueberry morning, N.Y.C. winds gusting wild and free
threatening Superman, Spongebob Squarepants and Smokey the Bear.
Snoopy keeps his eyes on the weather like a well-trained astronaut.

Yes, the balloons will fly, but tethered on long ropes
sometimes high as fifty-five feet, but held closer to earth today
by marching clowns determined not to let them fly away.
Alas, Ronald McDonald suffered a gash in his long left leg
quickly rushed to balloon hospital, no need to pay.

Yes, the balloons will fly but will I?
I wonder how they are at fixing hearts? I have a hole in mine.
GriefShare classes warn of the dangers of flying solo
especially on holidays, actually almost any day,
but family and friends tethered me on strong ropes
of love, prayers and a parade of kindnesses.

Yes, balloons will fly and so will I
when Sinatra flies me to the stars
to let me see abundant spring
in Nerja, Jupiter and Mars.

⋘⋙

What lifts you higher in your spirit?

How Do I Not Make the Same Mistake Again?

How do I not make the same mistake again? Like yesterday. I dropped my credit card because I had failed to put it back in its own spot like I always do. Now it was after service hours at the dealership. I had misread the time. A kind man came to our rescue, found my keys, took my card for payment, and I signed. I picked up my purse, sunglasses, phone, package, sweater, the receipt and probably my card. My grandson saw me safely back in my car and drove away.

I have never, ever left a card! I always put it back immediately! Except yesterday. Twenty-five minutes later at the gas pump, no card to put in the slot. Filling my car has been a major hurdle this year. I couldn't ask my car to return to the dealership as it was GAS...ping.

I found the number, and a friendly voice said she would look, but she had to find someone who could open the service window first. It began to rain on my just-washed car. "The 'Empty' light was winking at me, so I didn't even have the air on. No card. So sorry." I pleaded my case, wondering if I had dropped it by my car, by any chance, from my overflowing arms. She kindly agreed to go look in the parking lot.

Thunder! A rainbow! Thank you, Lord. I hadn't seen a rainbow all of our long hot summer. Just back from two weeks in the glorious mountain air, I was gasping too! Finally she returned with good news. Someone had turned in my card! But by now it was closing time, so I explained I couldn't get there until 1:00 tomorrow. I used my debit card, saluted the rainbow, stopped at Wendys for a single patty and a cold frosty, and came home in the rain for a late supper.

How not to repeat my mistakes? A string on my finger? A rubber band for my wrist? I'm going to look for a rainbow sticker for my wallet. I understand that forgetfulness increases with age, but friends often comment on my excellent memory. Memorizing helpful Bible verses has been a habit for a long time. I know that must help in daily life. But someone has quipped, "Life is so daily!"

CʒꙄ

What could help you remember all those details?

Is Charlie Brown Right?

A sunny Sunday ten of us who had shared stories and tears were invited to a comfortable condo with our peace offering as our community was emerging from the now four-month lockdown. Four of the class were unable to join us. We had to Zoom the several last sessions and missed the final supper at the church. Thankfully all had remained well, so we dared to come wearing smiles instead of masks.

Stories of hopes and hobbies, faith and fears circled the room. When asked, I described my cup as three-quarters full; the leader seemed pleased. I didn't mention yet that I was trying to write about this sudden change in my life as a praying friend had asked me to do. It is difficult and painful to attempt to put on paper anything that could help someone else thrown overboard to tread water and eventually swim to shore.

Our kind and sensitive leaders had invested thirteen weeks to help our little group navigate this new single state. A second volunteer couple also came who sponsored the fall group and did long-range planning. Our hostess, Sarah, had a thoughtful plan to express our appreciation and give these new friends gift certificates for local dining. They had asked us good questions with discussions of the helpful video series and workbook. This same format is effectively offered all over the country. I had been told I should go and I'm glad I did. Sometimes it was very difficult, but I also made new friends whose circumstances are similar. So, we have been encouraging each other and meeting when we could. Sarah introduced me to lavender lemonade, taking me to our local Lavender Fields for my first birthday without my boyfriend since college days.

Ham biscuits, shrimp and cake star at almost every Southern party. It seemed like an oxymoron to call it a "grief party" but that's what it was. We agreed we would like to meet again but have had to postpone until the new now. This very diverse group makes it particularly interesting. All of us have experienced cancellations of plans carefully made to see us through this first year. One man had to change his wife's memorial service and it is still unclear when he can reschedule. We are not the famous *Ship of Fools* but a Ship of Friends in unfamiliar waters.

My neighbor and I had planned a small patio supper to celebrate our husbands' birthdays tonight. But most were not ready to venture out. So, we cancelled the caterer and cautiously chose to dine where our men would have particularly enjoyed dinner. All precautions have been taken, and we also hope to see local businesses survive. Here's to toasting our wonderful memories with our husbands!

If you find yourself alone after a long difficult illness watching your loved one die or suddenly single, you can never be completely prepared for the shock to your system and a new-found confusion. It is frightening! All of the "D" words come to haunt you: discouraged, despair, doubt, dismay, disturbing, disoriented. Some days you don't know yourself. The evenings are endless and lonely and your bed even lonelier. Cooking has lost its charm or you don't know how, as several of the men have lamented. But one of our brave guys even successfully made lasagna like his wife always did for their family.

Everyone tells you, please see your doctor, following orders and suggestions. Do! Temporary help may be needed to sleep. I invented a mental *Trivial Pursuit* game, made countless lists, and bossed everyone. Friends who knew me well were genuinely worried about my wellbeing. As was my local family. Our son sat in with me when he took me to my doctor. I admitted to both that I had given everyone every reason to be very concerned. I would have been a perfect case study of a person in shock for a medical or psychology student. There are of course lots of alternatives to food preparation: drive-ins, contactless delivery, frozen entrees, but you will still be eating alone. Everything was complicated by the lock-down due to the mysterious virus; the schools, libraries, movies, gyms, museums, churches closed. We even wore masks when walking alone.

Try to eat what's healthy and find an understanding friend. Joan had been alone a year and warned me how difficult it was going to be, and it was! She even went with me to one *GriefShare* session for support. We would share whatever we had for dinner several nights a week in the beginning. Mingling salty tears in our soups. We did pretty well except for Pringles...actually any kind of chips would do. We even bought little measured portions and then ate two each with our wine. My doctor had told me I was low in sodium; what a great excuse! However, we were very disciplined about the wine. Some nights we watched TV and even fell asleep in our comfy chairs before it was time to go home and turn on our electric blankets.

03&0

Have you seen a doctor recently?

Life's Puzzle

One-way streets
two-faced people
three point turn
four-way stop signs
five egg whites
six lanes each way
seven-mile construction
eight-mile tunnel
nine miles deer crossing
ten minutes late
road work
expect delays
double fines in work zones
one-lane bridge
next exit closed
rest stop under repair
power failure
Coke machine out of order
new traffic circles
yield to oncoming traffic
too fast
too slow
avalanche zone
watch for falling rocks
no left turn
no right turn
bridges freeze first
lookout point
no re-entry
don't feed the bears
mask up
social distance
wash hands
Zoom tomorrow

Chapter Four

How Do You Keep the Music Playing?

When I first met George,
and through most of our early life together,
music came on vinyl discs played on a record
player with an arm and needle.

During the various stages of our lives,
those methods of playing changed to
tapes, compact discs, and walkmans,
and the equipment to play them
all required different batteries.

Now it's all recorded on my cell phone,
just like my memories of George.

D-E-A-T-H

Bob told us he would be healed. He and Barbara did everything right healthwise. We prayed for his restoration so we could have more fun dinners together with rich conversations. He wanted us to know ahead of time, and he was healed, completely, when the Lord took him to heaven, the ultimate healing. Barbara was devastated. He was so young. We cried for our friends.

We invited her to come to Canada for a week's breather before she faced her new reality. Each morning over strong coffee she and I developed an acrostic on the word death and painfully worked our way through it day by day. And now it is my new reality. She calls me frequently and says she prays for me every day.

D--Death is a door you never want to enter. It swings shut behind you with a heavy thud. Like the famous painting of Jesus waiting at the door by the artist William Holman Hunt, it cannot be opened from the outside. You can never go back to say goodbye, or apologize, or ask questions, or confess your feelings, or say I love you.

You can talk about regrets in *GriefShare* sessions, if you can even talk at all about your feelings. Otherwise it is like a door on a vault and you don't know the combination.

E--This one-way door is eternal. Nothing can ever change or ease its weight. No amount of prayer, pleading, or patience can alter the bitter truth. My husband used to serve as an MC at numerous conferences for businessmen and their wives. A weekend away in a comfortable hotel. The first morning at breakfast he would ask the guests, "How many of you said I love you to your spouse already this morning?" Maybe a quarter of the hands were raised. The second morning, same question, often three quarters of the room looked pleased with themselves, then he added, "How many of you said I love you more out of fear than of passion?" Tell your partner every single day how much you love, appreciate, and enjoy being with them. You may never get another chance. I didn't.

A--Acceptance of this new reality is not optional. We can weep, wail, deny and despair but it is a fact that someone is left alone. Years ago leaving the lake home of a couple we had spent great times with, the new widow took each of our hands and said earnestly, "Take good care of each other." Thankfully we always did.

T--Trust that God knows your future. If you don't know God well enough yet to trust him, you find yourself more alone than you ever imagined was possible. But the good news is that God is looking for you. Not because he does not know where you are but so that you can find out where you are. Totally alone! And he is waiting for you. The Good Shepherd is looking for his lost sheep.

H--Heaven is an absolute. As the little boy's popular book declares, *Heaven Is For Real.* Countless stories abound about where, how far, and is there golf in heaven like Billy Graham reputedly asked his dear Ruth. We could make heaven a study for the rest of our lives and never understand this mysterious dimension of reality. But more than ample proof exists that what the Bible claims about man's relationship to God is decided in this life. Then we spend eternity with or without God.

Without God?

Without trees, flowers, mountains, sunsets, oceans, sunrises, rainbows, birds, animals, families, food, friends, music, art, books, travel? Many of us who claim to be Christians have been very poor representatives of his love for all that he created. Of course, I know that there are books, artists and travelers who care nothing for the Eternal God Almighty. But where did they find language and color and continents? Pastor Andy Stanley sagely asks, "Who goes to heaven? Good people? Bad people? No. Forgiven people."

The good book will tell you how to find God, and, hopefully, as Hallmark cards say, you have a friend who is a beautiful blend of caring, sharing and love. God is love even when your loved one dies.

❧❧

With whom can you talk about death?

Second Guessing

Checking the dictionary for the actual definition of *second guessing*, I found that it was first used in the press and dictionary in 1941. The correct definition is "when you make a decision and start to think about it a little more and decide another decision might have been better." Remembering we were deeply involved then in WWII was interesting. A time of turmoil, anxiety, worries, uncertainty about the future, and grief over all the deaths. We could say the same thing is still true in our lives today. Plus that this current unprecedented time of fear and limited activity keeps us more separated from one another.

I expect everyone has studied their closet and wondered what to wear, or stood in front of a well-stocked fridge and asked, what was I after? Did I take dinner out of the freezer? Did I turn on or off the oven, start the washing machine, sprinkler, light, oven, hose, iron? Did I let the dog out, put the garbage on the curb or the package out for pick-up? Did I pay that bill, miss appointments or leave my friend waiting in the coffee shop? You could make your own list and know that you have second-guessed yourself. And I'm sorry to say that it only seems to get worse when we suddenly live alone.

What about products that say, "Do not use if open." That's the trick! How to get it open? We appreciate efforts for health and safety, but somewhere along the way we lose some of the strength in our hands. I have used rubber grippers, banged bottles on a hard edge, or held under hot water, all to no avail. Even the little paper circles inside of screw tops often break before they get the seal open. Plastic containers snap shut and mock me when I cannot pry them apart. My first purchase was an electric wine bottle opener. It works great once I pry the foil off, but I cannot squeeze the top foil tight enough to cut through for the opener to be placed on the cork. So I go at it with a sharp knife. Ouch!

Some widows report that they talk to their deceased partners, to themselves or family pets, only to search the lonely silence. Apparently Alexa can be trained to do more than wake me up, turn on the light, and give me the weather report, but she can't open a wine bottle or give me warm hugs.

☙❧

Relax, everybody does it. But indecision is a hindrance to your progress.

Trivial Pursuit

In some ways I feel like I'm in a *Trivial Pursuit*. Other days it's *Monopoly*. Go to jail! *Parchessi* sends me home. *Scrabble* describes the week. Each month is a *Chess* game. I haven't a *Clue* to where this year has gone. Board games must have been created by widowers--Is that plural for both men and women alone?

The ordinary routines of daily life seem to consume so much time. The *GriefShare* handbook states that your partner did at least fifty details, and now it's your turn. I knew I could put out the garbage and bring in the mail, but I never thought about the sprinklers that wouldn't turn off or the roof that leaked yesterday. And the car battery that failed again at the safety check after it was repaired last month. Two new tires needed, what brand to buy, then another half day to have them aligned. Bird feeders to fill, checks to write, leaves to blow, power washing and not enough time to read like I did before.

I don't feel sorry for myself. I am very thankful that my great guy didn't have to cope with COVID. It is just frustrating to me that I have lost my timing, reduced efficiency, and compromised organization. In my desk window I see a large spider who I can't decide if he is caught in his own elaborate web or if he is waiting for a victim. I have withdrawn from several activities that were so enjoyable and educational but time-consuming into my own little web. I do not consider myself to be a victim.

The great blessings of family here and distant, caring friends, health, home, happiness fill my life. I pray to be a balanced woman able to cope with the complications of life as they present themselves. The weekly Bible studies are where we hone skills, help, and encourage each other. Aqua Aerobics keep us breathing deeply, and meditation time with scripture is refueling for each day.

Anyone for *Chinese Checkers*?

CS80

I like to be organized, so I can be flexible. I call it "organized flexibility."

Cemetery in Kiev

Larger in death than in life---
granite statues line an avenue of accomplishment.
Darkened by decades of godless diatribe,
crosses bristle on many stone monuments
and sightless eyes are fixed on the past.

A conductor with upraised baton waits for the final chord,
the actress with blood-red roses dying on her breast,
the general at attention to review his troops,
the politician's last promise forgotten.
A composer bent over an unyielding keyboard,
the writer's pen laid down without words,
the youth who never knew manhood,
his mother weighted with tears of stone.
Lovers straining to embrace,
husband and wife, silent as time.

A morning mist hangs in the trees like grief.
Autumn leaves slick the street and rustle memories
in corners of the past, memorial wreaths curl into dust,
ribbons fade and roll away like dreams.

Closer in death than in life---
little space breathes betweens the busts of great and greater.
Was this their desire to parade their fortune before the living,
chiseled dates of birth and death until
winter rain erases name and fame?
Under black umbrellas we tiptoe tangled paths
where no one is left to remember the weeds.

Death knows no orchestra or audience.
Death cancels military parades and political promises.
Death silences all music and artistic acclaim.
Death steals the hope of youth and joy of motherhood.
Death defies a kiss or conversation.

+++

If Christ has not been risen
your faith also is in vain...
I Corinthians 15

And the Dog Died...

Why? Because he knew his young mistress was about to leave home to further her career in a distant city? He seemed playful as ever, gleefully helping unwrap the tissue from her gift bags. And *why* did my car not even growl when I was leaving to join the family for the last dinner so I could say goodbye to her?

Whoever heard of corroded battery wires in a car that has been garaged and pampered all of its young life? And *why* did the post office not return my mail on the designated date after my trip? And *why* does Netflix continue to offer me a free one-month trial when I have been a member for years? And *why* did the catalogue not honor my request for an exchange? And *why* did my great friend and pastor die way too young just when I needed his counsel and encouragement?

Why must be the most overworked word in the English language. Whatever happened yesterday? is the wrong question. I learned a long time ago and am still trying to remember to ask, instead, *how* do I deal with this effectively? I do have great memories and pictures of my granddogs. Actually three of them from two different families must be racing across green fields now and maybe playing with my husband, along with our three dogs who would have welcomed him by sight.

I'm convinced that the Creator who made so many kinds of amazing animals must have a place for them in Paradise. He who promised that the lion will lie down with the lamb has so many wonders for us to see if we just hold on to Him like I held onto the elephant whose ears chafed my bare legs as a little girl at the zoo, or the obstreperous camel who spit all the way down the Mount of Olives. But I'm not so sure I want to meet the cobra who was placed on my neck in Morocco.

How will we know our first grandson who died when but an infant? *How* old is he now? And does he know his grandparents and great grandparents? Does he look like his dad? I hope so!

So *how* do I make the best use of my time in this total upheaval of the COVID-19 virus and of my second year alone? Not *why* did it happen? Not *Why* me? *Why* not me?

The Driveway Church

This hallelujah September morning I worshipped in the driveway church in our neighborhood. Not the first make-do gathering. We have participated in The Hole-in-the-Wall church in Spain, whispering in a small living room in Poland during martial law, an apartment kitchen in Hungary, a posh hotel in South Africa, sitting on the ground under an acacia tree in Kenya with Swahili-speaking people, and in impressive buildings that Chinese Christians have built with everyone pitching in. I didn't mean to name drop but to show the world-wide necessity of believers meeting together, desiring to worship Christ.

Today I took the requested lawn chair and mask, joined in praising under shady magnificent pines, copper beech and willows dancing to violin music. At the end of the sloping drive the lectern was a large garbage can graced with a long crushed green velvet altar cloth. Perfect height for the pastor with a laptop and mic for the at-home people to link in on Zoom.

Wherever believers gather can be a sanctuary. I have been thrilled to worship in some of the great cathedrals of Europe. Their awesome beauty does elevate my thoughts heavenward, but these small gatherings are reminders of the first century where the Lord served communion in an upper room in Jerusalem.

We too shared communion in cups which held bread in a sealed base and the wine in the easy-to-open top. "As often as you do these things you do show forth my death until I come again." One of the men found these cups online. A joy-filled morning.

Yet today, but three days later, I have been awash in tears off and on. The soft grey morning released buckets of heavy rain. I dressed to match my new butterfly umbrella passed on to me by my priest friend. She gives me all kinds of things in goodie bags, mostly with butterflies on greeting cards, napkins which she purchased somewhere in her well-traveled life. As I stepped out of my car, the umbrella would not open, so I was soaked through before I got inside the clubhouse for Bible study. We had a very meaningful class sharing acrostics on our own names with supporting verses of scripture which were helpful in this time of crisis.

My tears began to leak for the heavy concerns of health, family, social and political problems. Harder and harder like the rain. I got chilled. Tears again. Overwhelming sadness. More tears, and I am supposed to be the older, wiser teacher.

We often have tearful moments. And I think I am not easily depressed by the weather. Usually I can thank the Lord for welcome rain when it comes without wind and lightning. But today I just wanted to curl up and cry. As soon as I got home, a nightie, hot tea (and cookies) in bed. I slept for two hours. I was crying for myself and my friends. Especially the new widow of our beloved pastor as Lindy faces this memorial week for her husband. He was like a younger brother to us. Another cup. It is still raining outside. I changed appointments. I need to stay home for the evening.

I am alone fifteen months now without my personal captain. We have cruised in all kinds of weather. "The seas are dropping, Honey." I am trying to learn that tears still come in waves at unexpected times. I am so blessed to know many of the promises that the Eternal Captain gave us in the Bible Log. Do I really understand all of them? No. But can I believe all? Yes. Because of His proven ability to keep His promises. "I will never leave you or forsake you."

Some of His very best blessings are friends who love you even when the mascara runs. I haven't worn any for months. These friends are not all followers of Christ. Agnostics, atheists, and the undecided are every bit as kind. I learned that a long time ago when one morning a florist delivery man rang my doorbell. He assured me that the address really was correct. The enclosed card read, "Your voice didn't sound right this morning on the phone. Love, Shirley." I pray for that kind of sensitivity to others. From a loaf of homemade bread, card, call or invitation at unexpected times. Carmelina calls them "just because" gifts. Her recent surprise was a miniature pumpkin with a wire stem that said, "I can do all things through Christ who strengthens me."

○₃⅋○

After more than a year of COVID-19, some churches are opening. What does church mean to you? Or is church irrelevant?

Night Rider

Your cars were Cinderella's pumpkin, Aladdin's carpet,
Cleopatra's palanquin, Elizabeth's carriage, Ben Hur's chariot---
showroom shiny, Armor-alled, leather fragrant,
four on the floor, equipped with Jay Andre's radio,
how many, I'm not sure, but I remember them all.

From the library to Prince Castle,
the Planetarium, to the Ambassador Bridge,
North Avenue, Rosie Road, and Lake Shore Drive,
I've "stuck with you, kid" for millions of miles
over oceans and seas and four continents.
Buckingham Drive, Sarnia Road, Belmont,
Grandin Place, Calle de Ronda, Kings Park Crescent,
Pine Bark Lane, Hunt Club Drive, Jefferson's hundred---
all double car garages except one and two with none.

The years have sped by like the 500,
with us cheering them all,
incredible experiences, since you made the best offer ever---
"You plan and I'll pay."

Now after 64, plus 4 dating, the only thing
that has changed from General Motors,
to Mercedes, are the handsome Chryslers
that line our driveways.

And sometimes on dark and stormy nights,
I have a mysterious, bearded,
night rider.

How Do You Keep the Music Playing?

Tony Bennett sings it best. That perfect description of a healthy marriage. The wonderful lyrics of "How Do You Keep the Music Playing?" emphasize the necessity for couples to keep their joy and passion alive. Composed by Michel Legrand with lyrics by Alan and Marilyn Bergman for the 1982 film "Best Friends." It was one of three songs with lyrics by the Bergmans that was nominated for Best Original Song at the 55th Academy Awards. It is very true to life as they have been married since 1958 and writing music almost daily.

We have used that song in counseling people who have seen us always holding hands, a quick kiss in a quiet corner, or deferring to each other, as they see we have been happily married for so long. Of course it is true that we are always changing, but the knowledge that you are fully loved is too precious to let it slip away. It takes constant music. Do you ever sit in the candlelight and listen to old love songs? Together, of course.

Now I have to listen alone and tears slip down my face, but I remember that *American in Paris* album was his first gift to me in college. I wondered if he was sending a message with "Our Love is Here to Stay." I didn't know it then but I do now. And we were "The Folks who Live on the Hill," "It had to be You," "I'll be Loving You Always." "Chicago" where we danced on State Street on New Year's Eve. And always when I get on a plane I sing to myself "Fly Me to the Moon." Those are sweet tears.

I hope you know what I mean. "What are you doing the rest of your life?" Young love through mature love to well-seasoned love needs music all the way through. You've no doubt seen couples sharing a table that seldom seem to speak. We often played a game of giving each other clues of hotel rooms or restaurants such as "under a green striped awning." If one could guess the place on the first clue, that was a winner. If it took three or more clues there was a penalty chosen by the other "best friend."

And George had a bond with dear Joan over music. One would start singing an old song and see if the other could join in with remembering all of the words. Now she starts my mornings with a song.

And it's not just pop songs that we enjoyed, but opera could move us both to tears. And my boyfriend taught me how to appreciate jazz. The improvisation, rhythm and variations on a theme. And he would listen carefully to my poetry. There are a lot of similarities. He was my comma man. He always wanted more commas in the text. He was often right.

Hymns of the faith that we had been learning since childhood, and newer gospel music were a source of worship and celebration. Bill Gaither has been the most prolific modern composer of music with sound messages. Brooklyn Tabernacle Choir, Hillsong, and so many others. "Amazing Grace" and "Because He Lives," bring me to consider the Lord's palpable presence.

Sinatra sings that "love is lovelier the second time around." That can be true for those widowed while quite young, but for those whose arms have been intertwined for decades, the sweet memories are more than enough.

CBED

Google the lyrics to "How Do You Keep the Music Playing?" Write them here.

Lindy Dear

From Willowbank to Williamsburg to Nerja to Israel and home again,
crossing oceans, climbing mountains, counting blessings.
We have traveled many miles of God's green earth
over a quarter century that seems like yesterday.
Prayed eyes wide open during countless rainbow sunrises,
praised in wonder over God's signature sunsets,
danced with joy down Pintada tented with stars,
shared lumumbas and laughter memories in the sand,
cried in each others' arms circled within the prayers of friends;
And now the world has turned again and time seems suspended.

You and your darling daughters
surrounded by a great cloud of witnesses
embracing the Lord's amazing provisions,
yearning to understand His plan,
practicing obedience and patience,
finding light in the increasing darkness
are more loved than you can possibly know.
Your family ministry to shepherd the sheep
has gathered thousands of us into the sheepfold until
the Son rises with healing in His wings
to gather all around the throne of grace
rejoicing with the Heavenly Host.
Alegria

CR&O

Write a note to a grieving friend.

If I Were In Paris

If I were in Paris on this autumn afternoon
I would walk alone in the Bois de Boulogne
listening for rustling in the leaves, warning
sound of fear, like the breath of a bullet past my ear.
I would go to Notre Dame and weep at our Lady's feet...
Praying that the God who knows the hearts
of all men, women and fatherless children
would pour His healing over the fractured city
like the tireless bells of the cathedral.
The Parisians have suffered wars and rumors
of wars until life became eat, drink, and be merry
for today we die...
Back on the left bank searching book seller stalls
I'd buy all the Bibles and give them away so the grieving
could know there is hope for a better day.
Stopping for coffee at a café I know that Camus and Sartre
had no answers for today.
Philosophers and politicians have no weapons against
satanic evil rooted in the hearts of terrorists...
November has blighted the buds
in the gardens of the Tuileries,
even tea is no longer warm at the Ritz,
Mona Lisa keeps her secret vigil behind closed doors,
The Eiffel Tower is bandaged in a bloodied flag,
and Rodin's Gates of Hell are shaking...

Chapter Five

Does God Use Email?

My computer requires a battery that can be recharged.
It is different from my iPad, and my cell phone.

I wonder if God has a computer.
Surely it doesn't require all these different batteries!

And what kind of computer does God have to control seasons,
tides, sunsets...so NASA can put astronauts in space?

Aren't you glad you'll never hear these words from
God:

BFF

You know how it is on a sunny Saturday morning at a church ladies' breakfast, you meet someone new and you just *know* you need to know her. In 2002 it was just such a day when we were introduced. And we knew. Plans quickly developed for get-acquainted lunches, then dinner with husbands, Monday morning coffee, scripture reading, discussion and prayers. She even packed up on very short notice when she hardly knew me and went to Spain with me for three weeks while I was writing *Have You Met Eve?*

Susan and I have traveled together, just we two, then with husbands, stateside and overseas. That is a true test of friendship. We zig and zag together extremely well. We love each other but manage to conduct separate lives, many different friends, and are seldom on the phone. We are all blessed with a variety of priorities and responsibilities, texting mostly just times for when to meet again. But sadly, she was not able to come to our memorial service due to her own health issues. I believe the Lord protected her from additional sorrow as I know she loved my George like a brother.

One evening in the shadow of the magnificent Cathedral in Seville I asked Chris seriously if he would be my brother since I have no siblings and no living parents. Our wise pastor had suggested that we should ask one another to serve as family members if we felt alone. Not only did Chris accept but they have adopted me as family, including me so many happy times. When George was alive we did all kinds of things exploring together. And they were nothing if not enthusiastic! At a special restaurant in Carmona, the congenial waiter finally said to Chris, "You don't talk!"

On New Year's Eve we have celebrated the coming years together with our overnight home and homes. What a wonderful way to start the New Year together with reminiscing evenings by the fire, special breakfasts and prayers. I have my overnight bag packed and am feeling so blessed.

Sometimes I am invited to stay overnight after a Perdue game or late evening in Susan's B and B. Almost always I accept.

Thank you, Lord, for friends who knew me in happier days and love me still.

ϢϣϠ

Send a card to your best friend...just because.

Susan Jane's B&B

Susan Jane's B&B rests comfortably by Powhatan Creek
reservations advised as it is often full as the cookie jar.
Happy hour lingers until sunset blushes the sky
spritzers on the back deck sparkling as conversation
books, travel, church, politics, history, blessings.
Sentinel trees heard thanksgiving for a passing pastor
Susan's miracle health and my 64th anniversary,
lessons learned through sunshine and sorrow.
Evening quieted a hallowed hush for true Southern dining
ham loaf, green beans, mashed potatoes, lemon chess pie,
Susan's delectable baking her generous signature.
The blue and yellow guest room, with teacup night lights
last shared with my love, swaddles me in memory
floating on sheets the color of favorite Canadian Lakes.
When dawn gilded the skies, I crept to the deck
to find the master of the house ready to serve
a fragrant pot of tea and soft plaid shawl,
I know he misses my husband keenly.
Birds sang good morning, even a great blue
graced us with a salute over the garden.
Susan awakened from much-needed rest,
produced the best buttermilk blueberry pancakes ever.
The creek mirrored the Patriarchs as we read scripture
prayerfully, our favorite Monday mornings.
I'm already looking forward to our next home and home.
Thank you, dearest friends.

൬ൈ

What do you expect from a best friend?

Thanksgiving Day

Today is the day, November 26 in the United States. In Canada where we spent many happy years, it is celebrated the second Monday in October. Google tells me there are fifteen other countries that observe their own version of Thanksgiving. Some celebrate colonial migrations to the Americas, others the start of a new lunar cycle to welcome the harvest season.

Ronald McDonald was successfully repaired from the ripping winds last year and, along with a few of the other favorites that were willing to fly without the cheering crowds of previous years, bravely flew over the deserted sidewalks of Macy's N.Y.C. The faithful watched from the safety of their homes and probably prayed for the control of the COVID scourge of 2020.

The much-loved dog show from Philadelphia showcased all previous winners, and the stadium seats were filled with pictures of the ticket holders or their dogs. Even the football games suffered many turnovers, fumbles, and cancellations.

We all were disappointed at the restrictions that the virus spawned, but American families once again rose to the occasion. Some of us ordered take-out dinners in support of local favorite restaurants. This service has risen as high as homemade rolls and Mom's apple pie. But the empty chairs were filled with treasured memories and conversations centered around missing dear ones. I was invited for a glass of cheer with friends who have adopted me and miss my boyfriend almost as much as I do.

A sweet afternoon interlude as I waited for our son's family to come to me. They all have helped me make it through this dreaded "second year" with thanksgiving, peace and joy. You cannot do it all by yourself. There are so many people who need a friendly face to talk to. And I am especially blessed to have so many precious friends after living here twenty-five years. They pick me up or invite me to join them on numerous occasions.

Our children need to be reminded of the countless blessings we enjoy. Some of our schools no longer emphasize the providence of God in leading our brave ancestors to these freedom shores. Author George Santayana wrote, "Those who cannot remember the past are condemned to repeat it."

We count our blessings and thank you, Lord God.

Paper Chase

Google tells me the term originally meant, "The effort to earn a diploma or college degree, especially in law, or a professional certificate or license." Decades after college graduation I find myself daily in a paper chase. Being a writer exacerbates my problem. Piles of poems, stacks of folders, miles of manuscripts, study notes and outlines, newspapers, magazines, grocery lists, bills, receipts, letters to answer, books to savor, gift bags, tissue paper and note cards.

I consider myself a well-organized person but somehow it doesn't apply to paper. It drifts around the house like mounds of autumn leaves, tucks in the corners and under pillows. You may not see it, but I know it's there waiting for me under the throw.

My father was a newspaper owner/editor and I've always said I had ink in my veins, but I wish it found its way to the proper paper more easily. Then I could settle in the library with my next book. There are even books I would like to reread as well as new, but time is cluttered with papers that need to be sorted.

And then there are distractions. A young buck apparently four years old is nosing through the piles of bronzed leaves, just beyond my desk windows. He limps painfully, and the rack on his left side is missing. He too has lost something terribly important that cannot be replaced. It must have been a dreadful fight with a more powerful opponent. I wonder if he had a partner and any family to snuggle close at night and tell stories. Or if he has stumbled along for years by himself. He helps me keep things in perspective. A paper chase is of little consequence compared to his problem.

I can ask Alexa to play Claude Debussy while I consider what to keep and what to discard. Now that I don't have family meals to prepare I can usually set aside a little time in the late afternoon with a cup of spicy tea and the next book. I have a candle with this CS Lewis quote that says, "You can never get a cup of tea large enough or a book long enough to suit me."

CRO

What are you currently reading?
What are the titles of the last five books you've read?
Do you watch more than four or five hours of T.V. a day?

Thanksliving

I was surprised to learn that this energizing term first appeared as a typo in a church bulletin years ago. It is a gift. I often keep it written on my chalkboard in all seasons.

In this bountiful time of family and friends we find ourselves restricted again more severely as the dreaded virus marches at random around our God-blessed America. The promise of vaccines soon is hopeful, but distribution is a political football in this season when we don't even know which team has the ball, or how many family members can tailgate together. It is getting too cold for picnics. Shops and restaurants are still limiting customers. Fashion masks or angry slogans are the newest must have. We don't know who to believe. Even our media are compromised. And we are becoming suspicious and mean spirited.

The Virginia woods are burnished russet, gold and red as we shop for our Thanksgiving feasts in hopeful anticipation. It is difficult to know how to plan. For the first time we ordered our meal to be prepared to reheat at home in an effort to help our favorite restaurant survive after the masks come off, or will they? Some predict this may be the new way to live in America, like in Asia. So, no tantalizing aromas from the kitchen on Thursday. I picked up our meal for four today. Take-out packaging that can be reheated in the oven must be the hottest item at Target.

Several years ago I decided to focus on Thanksliving because we are so blessed in this country, but it has gotten more difficult. Prayer requests keep pouring in, but my phone dings often with the reassurance that friends are praying for each other. We share encouraging scripture verses daily. "Blessed are those who know the passwords of praise." I try to offer those passwords which are infinitely more important than the passwords of our locked-up lives. "Holy Holy Holy." Blessed Trinity. God Almighty. My Savior, Redeemer, Shepherd, Friend, I magnify, exalt, esteem, extole You. I like to sing my way into His Presence with some of the old hymns and new praise songs. "Down at your feet, O Lord."

Yesterday just as I was into my morning devotions, my phone received a **HELP** call from a neighbor at the top of the street. I pulled on a sweat suit, skipped makeup and earrings (I feel totally unprepared without earrings). Another car was in her driveway, no answer to the doorbell, circled windows, staircase empty, she hadn't fallen down there, no car in the garage. Hurried to the police at our neighborhood gate. A second message with her request explaining that she was quarantined out of town with her son. Then the sinking realization that it was another scam, and I had opened her cry for help. But I would do it again. I don't know how to tell the difference when the name is a friend who might very well call me for help. As I returned home, her car was open in the driveway and full of groceries for the feast. We were so glad to see each other but quickly realized it would mean changing our email passwords. That strains my Thanksliving!

The land line at home announced that the Christmas order I had placed three days ago (time consuming) could not be processed since my credit card was refused. "Please call customer service." Taking care of more of the fifty things that are now my responsibility, I left the call for later. I am thankful I can do these extra things; they just take time. And I have lots of time.

Every customer in the country must have been being served, as I ate my solitary supper with the speaker on. A friendly voice kept reminding me how important my call was to them. Now I have been waiting so long I don't want to give up my place in the invisible line, so I climb into bed with my book, catalogue grinning up at me, the offending airline credit card, and coffee, volume turned low on the necessary phone reminders. Thanksliving?

Finally, much later, a strong male voice (that speaks English) answers and begins the search through endless numbers but he sadly tells me there is no order in my name. Then he remembers that on the Saturday when I ordered, they were having trouble with their computer service. But if there is no order, why was my card refused? Anyway we begin the arduous journey through these happy, smiling pages as we reconstruct my order. It is one of those catalogues that has things for everyone on your list, lots of little items that are fun and useful. My customer server earned his title (I think he was number five on the extensions menu). By now we are old friends, chatty, wondering if I'll get two such orders delivered. It won't be a problem, just call...

☙❧

List ten things for which you are thankful.

71

Asolo

Robert Browning after the death of his Elizabeth,
married only fifteen years

The last breath of winter sharp as a new knife blade,
cutting as his aunt saying
you've added a stone or two since I last saw you,
as cruel as his irreplaceable loss,
so he fled again to Asolo.

Leaving the shimmering city,
a jeweled brooch on the breast of the sea,
intoxicating perfume of vineyards embraced him.
The carriage horses glistened and snorted
protesting the steep climb into the hills,
joyous wedding music gracing the long green lawns.
Finally settled into his favorite rooms of the villa
he sighed in sorrowful memory,
slept and dreamt of her.

Refreshed and resolute he took the walking stick for
his morning constitutional and, as always, pens and journal
in a well-seasoned gray leather satchel.
Warm family memories in Florence and Siena,
sweet companions.

But Asolo was his favorite retreat.
He selected a particular table at the Village Square
Coffee Shop, ordered it hot and strong
perhaps laced with brandy.

Would he ever be able to say again
God's in his heaven,
all's right with the world?

Does God Use Email?

"I havE comE that you might havE lifE and havE it morE abundantly."

"For God so lovEd thE world that hE gavE his only bEgottEn son that whoEvEr bEliEvEs in him shall havE EtErnal lifE."

"I and thE FathEr arE onE. If you bEliEvE in God, bEliEvE in mE. In my FathEr's housE arE many mansions. If it wErE not so I would havE told you and if I go I will comE again and rEcEivE you unto mysElf that whErE I am you will bE too."

These are just three of the thousands of Emails that God sends every day and night worldwide. Have you never heard His whisper in the long dark night? He smiles on you at sunrise and reassures you every sunset that He watches you all through the night. It doesn't take a sermon or even a Bible if you know the little song "Jesus Loves Me, This I Know." When asked what his favorite song was, the famous opera star, Jerome Hines, said it was this children's song. It is a fact that some dictatorships have used this song, substituting their leader's name for Jesus. Scripture declares that there is no other name whereby you can be saved for all eternity. Sing it over and over until you believe it's true. Then listen for the little bell that tells you God is calling again. He promises to even pray for you by his Holy Spirit if you will just wait and listen for his wisdom. He loves you so much that He will move heaven and earth to get your attention.

Look up! "Every cloud is a flag to His faithfulness" to show you the way. Every leaf a creation of His hand to dry your tear, every star a light for you to find your way to take the next step.

If thE Son makEs you frEE, you shall bE frEE indEEd.

⊂⊃⊃⊂⊂

Have you heard from God recently? Have you responded?

Croquembouche and Candles

Invitations usually went out in late November for our festive Christmas Dessert and Coffee party. It became a tradition for our friends and neighbors to chat over a sliver of cake, and then easily move on for another cup of coffee. They knew to just have a bowl of soup before they came to spend the evening. A very fluid party with time to talk with everyone. Mark, at five, was the butler and Julie, at seven (and for many years thereafter), showed them where to put their coats. We served punch and no punch with little baskets of roasted, salted pecans strategically scattered.

When the candles lit the dessert table, the guests found Cherries Jubilee, cheesecake, Lemon Angel, a meringue as large as a silver tray, mounded with cream and strawberries, chocolate cake with tiny candy canes crossed all around the sides, coconut pie and--just one year--croquembouche. It was beautiful! A glistening tower of tiny filled cream puffs within golden strands of caramelized sugar. I had sugar streamers from one end of the kitchen to the other! So, I told everyone to enjoy now but there would never be a repeat. All of those other desserts were fun to do!

We loved to entertain in all kinds of ways. A chili party was welcome in January for just eight to ten in the dining room. Little bowls of sour cream, chopped onion, and shredded cheddar at each end. For Valentines Day I enjoyed doing a ladies lunch for women alone. Again this year I invited only widows and we shared our stories and a few tears in our tea.

March was birthday month for both children and every year we tried to do a different theme. One of the boys' best was a moon trip to the planetarium and moon pizza crust at home afterward.

April and May usually blossomed with showers, weddings and babies. June was full of family celebrations with Mother's Day and Father's Day and both of our birthdays.

July was Dominion Day, The Fourth, picnics and Bar-B-Ques. Our backyard had lost an enormous tree whose trunk became the base of a huge round table, topped with a lazy susan and a round bench that our ingenious carpenter built. That was the hardest piece of "furniture" to leave behind when we moved East.

August at the cottage we feasted on blueberries, peaches, and corn on the cob, and afterward a slow boat ride drifting close to the loons as they gathered their young with preparations for the long flight south. I can still hear their haunting cry.

September meant soups, stews, spaghetti suppers for casual evenings with friends.

October's bright blue weather colored the maples, oaks, beech, into an extraordinary palette for harvest time. Also turkey on the Weber became a regular feast, repeated at Christmas time. Our three generations of men have the timing down to a science. Since our family has both Canadians and U.S. citizens to celebrate our freedoms and founding under God, it is a special season of *Thanksliving* all autumn. I like to remember that not only is the United States "One nation under God" but the Dominion of Canada means "He shall have dominion from sea to sea." "United we stand, divided we fall."

I am so grateful for all the friends and family that have graced our tables all of these years. Some traditions are altered by necessity, others added. For many years I have enjoyed posing a question somewhere between dinner and dessert. "We are delighted that you could join us this evening. Now who would you like to add to our table for this evening's conversation? Male or female, living or dead, this country or another, anyone you would enjoy talking to." We have had all manner of people from the conductor of the Chicago Symphony, to Wall Street tycoons, Mother Teresa, Monet, Van Gogh, Golda Maier, dictators, and movie directors, Churchill and Roosevelt... and a number of their own grandparents. It always makes for a fascinating, different evening even with many of the same friends until the candles burn low.

CRQO

Who will you invite to share a sandwich with you? Call them today.

United We Stand

When distilleries make hand
sanitizers
Underwear manufacturers
masks
Soccer fields sport tent
hospitals
Auto manufacturers retool for
ventilators
We rightly applaud American
ingenuity.
But have we also forgotten
God's prescription
"To humble ourselves
and pray,
seek God's face,
turn from our wicked ways?"
Do we believe
"That He will hear from heaven
Forgive our sins
And heal our land?"

II Chronicles 7:14

Chapter Six

A Long Walk

*Let me live my days walking in grace
and truth before you.*

Dwindling Days

As Sinatra sang so wistfully about dwindling days, my private woods, exhausted from fanning summer's heat, now lie in heaps of burnished gold. But the fire of the two Japanese maples still burns by the porch and at the dining room window. Winter pansies wave from flower pots, the sharp white winter kale pokes the curly french purple cabbage. An angel beckons at the front door, and candles dance in every window.

The angel choir commands the dining room table and the Christmas tree on a pedestal is festooned with musical instruments and angels to make music everywhere. Alexa knows how to join in.

A crippled old reindeer leans against the library window watching for Santa, and the snowman doesn't melt on the kitchen bench. Mulled cider is simmering on the stove, and I have Christmas cookies to offer if you can stop in.

Neighbors knock with handfuls of homemade fudge and cookies. Surprise bags are on the front steps. Gift boxes of nuts and cookies arrive in the mail. And long-time friends invite me over to join them for supper. It is my pleasure to entertain several dinner guests in small groups and especially my local family several evenings as December slips away. Everyone is being very cautious but we need to see these smiling faces. Bumping elbows and knuckles is temporary. They will never replace hugs and kisses.

We are realizing never to take the small things as insignificant and to treasure the wondrous skies, stars, and Christmas moon. Every day and night is a testimony of God's watch care. We are well aware of how blatantly we have broken His commands and are praying daily for our country to return to our foundational values.

As the New Year arrives at our door I am full of thanksgiving for every blessing and seeking how best to be a comfort, companion, and counselor of joy to friends and family. Our *promise rings* are rock solid guarantees from the God of our universe. They promise to provide us with the strength, power and love that we so desperately need.

Electric Blanket, Lumumba and Alphabet

You will have sleepless nights. You will have restless nights. You will have lonely nights. Don't fight it even if you have a busy day lined up for tomorrow. Some read, others watch T.V. The most industrious get up and clean a room.

I turn on my blanket if it is cool before I crawl in against a wall of pillows with warm memories. A hot lumumba in a tall glass would be wonderful to take with me if I were in Spain watching the moon over the Mediterranean. The rich cocoa laced with brandy is surefire sleep. Named for the first prime minister of the independent Congo when it broke away from Belgium. Sadly it cost him his life for taking that stand. He was assassinated at only thirty-five. He left a devastated young son and a widow.

So I resort to the alphabet. When our first granddaughter was in a Christian school kindergarten she learned the alphabet with simple bible verses. She would proudly recite them at any opportunity. I thought if she could remember twenty-six verses I should be able to do the same.

I selected verses from the New Living Bible translation like "Because the Lord is my Shepherd I have everything I need." But I gave myself permission not to try to remember the references. Google can always find them. Try emphasizing every word in that phrase.

When I wake up and can't go back to dreamland I start down the letters. Seldom do I reach Z before I am zzzing again. The amazing thing to me is if I wake up again, I know where I left off, and I start there. If I do reach number twenty-six then I try to reverse the order. My alphabet is included. Or you could choose your own. This has been my best solution for sleeplessness for more than thirty years. It still works.

ೞ

What helps you sleep? What's the first thing you do when you wake up?

79

A. Romans 8:28 - "And we know all things work together for good if we love God and are fitting into his plans."

B. Psalm 23:1 - "Because the Lord is my shepherd, I have everything I need."

C. Psalm 37:5 - "Commit everything you do to the Lord. Trust him to help you do it and he will."

D. Matthew 5:17 - "Don't misunderstand why I have come; it isn't to cancel the laws of Moses and the warnings of the prophets. No, I came to fulfill them and make them all come true."

E. Psalm 119:147 - "Early in the morning, before the sun was up, I was praying and pointing out how much I trust in you."

F. Jeremiah 29:11- "For I know the plans I have for you," says the Lord, "they are plans for good and not for disaster, to give you a future and a hope."

G. John 3:17 - "God did not send his Son into the world to condemn it, but to save it."

H. Psalm 119:1-3 - "Happy are all who perfectly follow the laws of God; happy are all who search for God and always do his will, rejecting compromise with evil and walking only in his path."

I. Psalm 119:19 - "I am but a pilgrim here on Earth; how I need a map. Your commands are my chart and guide."

J. John 3:3 - "Jesus replied, 'with all the earnestness I possess I tell you this: unless you are born again you can never get it into the kingdom of God.'"

K. Romans 14:11 - "Every knee shall bow to me and every tongue confess to God."

L. Colossians 2:7 - "Let your roots grow down into him and draw up nourishment from him. See that you go on growing in the Lord; become strong and vigorous in the truth you were taught; let your lives overflow with joy and thanksgiving for all that he has done."

M. Psalm 128:5, 6 - "May the Lord continually bless you with Heaven's blessings as well as with human joys. May you live to enjoy your grandchildren! And may God bless Israel."

N. Ephesians 2:18 - "Now all of us, whether Jews or Gentiles, may come to God the Father, with the Holy Spirit's help because of what Christ has done for us."

O. Psalm 139:1 - "Oh, Lord, you have examined my heart and know everything about me."

P. Psalm 139:24 - "Point out anything you find in me that makes you sad, and lead me along the path of everlasting life."

Q. Psalm 141:6 - "Quick Lord! Answer me for I have prayed."

R. Psalm 106:4 - "Remember me, Lord, while you are blessing and saving your people."

S. Isaiah 55:6 - "Seek the Lord while you can find him; call upon him while he is near."

T. Proverbs 3:5, 6 - "Trust in the Lord with all thine heart and lean not unto thine own understanding."

U. John 16:9 - "The world's sin is unbelief in me."

V. John 15:5 - "Yes, I am the Vine; you are the branches. Whoever lives in me and I in him shall produce a large crop of fruit."

W. Psalm 68:19 - "What a glorious Lord! He who daily bears our burdens also gives us our salvation."

X. Psalm 42:11- "Expect God to act!"

Y. 1 Peter 1:8 - "You love him even though you've never seen him; though not seeing him you trust him, and even now you are happy with the inexpressible joy that comes from Heaven itself."

Z. Psalm 134:3 - "May the Lord bless you from Zion, the Lord himself who made Heaven and Earth."

CR80

Do you have a favorite Bible verse? Write it here.

Some Assembly Required

Gillis Lundgren is not a well-known name but he had world-wide fame as the promoter of flat-pack, assemble yourself furniture. IKEA's international fame developed from a day when he was frustrated trying to fit a small table in his compact post-war car to deliver for a photo shoot. "Why not take the legs off?" rang in his head like an opening bell. And he ran with it. Hired as the fourth employee of the fledgling Swedish company, his designs and packing ideas promoted the company into a multi-million-dollar operation that made fifteen Billy bookcases a minute. More than forty-one million had been sold by the company's thirtieth anniversary, all for you to assemble.

And parents know the familiar routine of 'making' bikes and trikes and trains and planes that are ready to go on Christmas morning. I especially had fun furnishing the doll houses. Good preparation for now when my life needs to be reassembled.

It cannot be accomplished all in one evening, or week or even a year. It includes how you think, how you act, where you go, how often, with whom and why. It is never static. It is never all finished and wrapped with a big bow. That is the challenge. But a good one, for none of us wants to be locked in a house of grief. The windows and doors need to be opened to include fresh air for family, friends and strangers.

We need a new mindset every morning.

Ralph Waldo Emerson is quoted as saying, "What lies behind you and what lies before you pales in comparison to what lies inside you." I believe that is true. But he is also quoted as saying, "I grieve that grief can teach me nothing, nor carry me one step into nature." I wish I could ask him about that because it seems to me if I don't learn anything from my grief then I die too. He apparently said that following his young daughter's death. Maybe it was too soon. I wouldn't like to just depend on what is inside of me. Every day brings new situations and solutions.

In the current novel *Five Wives* the statement is made, "If the pain is gone, so is the one you've loved. It means you've forgotten." If that is true then I expect to be in emotional pain until we meet again. But pain means I'm alive. Now what am I going to do about it?

Caring friends would say, "I'm so sorry you lost your husband. My standard reply at first was, "Thank you, I am too, but he's not lost or he didn't die, I did. And I know where he is." Presumptuous you say, but that is what the Bible reassures me.

Ten things I have learned from the grief of my husband's death:

1. I am not alone, for Jesus promised to never leave me nor forsake me.
2. I am learning to seek Him more diligently every day. From the music of the morning to the Carolina wrens on the feeder, the cinnamon warmth of my tea to the timeless Bible. I pan it for gold every day and record promises, always noting the conditions, seeking "a long obedience in the same direction" as Nietzsche wrote.
3. I also need to see friends who take me as I am and seem to love me anyway. In this year of masks and mystery we have had to be creative to see each other, but it has been possible from the opening of the garage wine bar in March to today's December Christmas gift exchange with Our Five outdoors in the warmth of the sun and nearby heat lamp. I gave my five the "Better Together" mugs from the TV show of the same name. We need each other.
4. I try to watch my step without his warm hand to hold. I often thought I was his security as his eyesight dimmed, but it started on our college campus where we always reached for each other. And now I realize more than ever how much he was my security. One hand for each other on this Love Boat.
5. I need to learn to ask for help. Perhaps the most difficult of all. It is a matter of pride to think I can manage this all by myself. I can't.
6. I want to stop more often to appreciate the little things from the first crocus in the snow to the eight trumpets as they blare from my Christmas Amaryllis.
7. I need siestas (not naps, naps are for babies and old people) most days but not if it means missing togetherness. Lying flat on my back is very relaxing and less likely to induce sleep. I begin by praying for as many concerns as the Holy Spirit brings to mind.
8. I love to read and absorb as many good books as possible.
9. I try to avoid "what if" questions and think in terms of "how now" do I deal with this. Someone nearby has the answers I need.
10. The Bible gives me the promised assurance that I will be reunited with my love for eternity. Hopefully, I will be wearing red.

A Long Walk

A beckoning bench, sometimes on a long walk I see a beckoning bench. It calls, "Come and stop a bit and look at all I can show you." Today is December 26, 2020, and as usual, my favorite winter chair by the "laughing fire" called me. Ruth Graham wrote about her "laughing fire" and that resonates with me. Often by the fire, reading scripture and listening to all kinds of music, it is as if the fire dries my sweetest tears and gives me back the glow of joy and laughter.

When I began this long walk alone, a praying friend asked me to record some observations on what my new life taught me. It was months before I could gather any thoughts to begin. Now I find I have gathered an armful of wild, wood-sweet blossoms and evergreens, and it is time to go home and find a vase of water.

Christmas beauty was everywhere on this crisp, polished day after we opened all of our love-gifts by our son's fire. Like most people we gathered on Facebook with extended family, feasted at candlelit tables, and prayed for an end to all the sufferings of separation. It was a joy-filled day and yes a few tears dried on our cheeks when his daughter presented a pictorial video of what her father taught her, all set to her original song. God, my heavenly Father, continues to teach me how to walk "by faith and not by sight."

Knowing that I did not want to ramble on and on (and friends would not want me to) I decided I must bring this last year's rambling to conclusion before I could begin a New Year's walk with my Savior. This is the vase of fresh water.

In my regular reading, I noticed a prayer at the end of Psalm 61. Recording it in my *promise ring*, I want to make it my prayer for the coming year. "Guard me God with your unending, unfailing love and let me live my days walking in grace and truth before you. And my praises will fill the heavens forever, fulfilling my vow to make every day a love gift to you."

CRWD

What are you learning about yourself?

I will be praying for you,
the readers, on my long walk.

May 2021

Acknowledgements

High Tide Publications
Founder-owner, Jeanne Johansen
consistently pursues high-water marks for High Tide Publications.
Her dedication and determined excellence result in
outstanding books of all genres.

Cindy L. Freeman, also an author,
shares the same high standards and service with her meticulous skill in
editing.

I am grateful for their attention to detail,
encouragement and friendship.

Scripture quotations from
The Living Bible
The Message
New American Standard Bible
The Passion Translation

About the Author

The intrigue of watching the printed word roll off the huge presses in her father's newspaper started Joyce's love of writing. She became the newspaper correspondent for her first grade class in Horace Mann School, Sedalia, Missouri. "Ink in her veins" flowed freely. In college, she was the literary editor of her school's prize-winning yearbook.

A member of the Poetry Society of Virginia, she has belonged to the National League of American Pen Women for more than forty years. She is also a charter member of the Williamsburg Poetry Guild.

Over the years, Joyce has circled the globe, mostly with her husband representing service organizations, meeting people where they are, discovering their needs, and helping them to maximize their resources.

She has served as an inspirational conference speaker, continues to teach two weekly Bible studies, and is always involved in community and church work.

George and Joyce were sweethearts at Wheaton College, married on graduation weekend. Hand-in-hand they celebrated life and faced challenges for sixty-four years. They are blessed with a daughter and son, their wonderful spouses, five grandchildren, and one great granddaughter.

Joyce has authored six previous books and a multitude of poems in all genres, but this book is the most personal of her work. A friend asked her to write about this new time in her life with the goal of encouraging others who are learning to live again after the death of a loved one.

Books by Joyce Carr Stedelbauer

Have You Met Eve?

Have You Seen the Star?

Who Rolled the Stone?

Where are You Adam?

The Awesome Alphabet Animals Party

The Angels Birthday Celebration

A new widow learns
Batteries Not Included
some assembly required

www.ingramcontent.com/pod-product-compliance
Lightning Source LLC
Chambersburg PA
CBHW030524100426
42813CB00001B/141